Infant/Toddler Caregiving

A Guide to

Routines

Janet Gonzalez-Mena

Developed by the

Center for Child and Family Studies

Far West Laboratory for Educational Research and Development

for the

Child Development Division

California Department of Education

Publishing Information

Infant/Toddler Caregiving: A Guide to Routines was developed by the Center for Child and Family Studies, Far West Laboratory for Educational Research and Development, San Francisco. (See the Acknowledgments on page viii for the names of those who made significant contributions to this document.) The document was edited for publishing by Sheila Bruton, working in cooperation with Peter Mangione, Janet Poole, and Mary Smithberger. It was prepared for photo-offset production by the staff of the Bureau of Publications, California Department of Education, under the direction of Theodore R. Smith. The layout and cover were designed by Steve Yee, and typesetting was done by Jeannette Huff.

The guide was published by the California Department of Education, 721 Capitol Mall, Sacramento, California (mailing address: P.O. Box 944272, Sacramento, CA 94244-2720). It was distributed under the provisions of the Library Distribution Act and *Government Code* Section 11096.

ISBN 0-8011-0877-2

Ordering Information

Copies of this publication are available for $8.25 each, plus sales tax for California residents, from the Bureau of Publications, Sales Unit, California Department of Education, P.O. Box 271, Sacramento, CA 95802-0271. Other publications that are available from the Department may be found on page 128, or a complete list may be obtained by writing to the address given above or by calling the Sales Unit at (916) 445-1260.

Photo Credits

The California Department of Education gratefully acknowledges the following individuals and organizations for the use of the photos that appear in this publication:

Sheila Signer, cover, pp. 1, 2, 5, 7, 9, 10, 11, 16, 17, 19, 21, 22, 24, 25, 32, 33, 34, 37, 38, 44, 45, 47, 54, 55, 56, 58, 59, 60, 65, 67, 72, 73, 74, 75, 77, 79, 84, 85, 95, 96, 105, 107, 110; Carol Wheeler, pp. 15, 86, 88; Fern Tiger Associates, p. 57.

Contents

MODULE II

Group Care

Infant/Toddler Caregiving: A Guide to Routines

Caregiving routines are opportunities for caregivers to build a close personal relationship with each child while attending to his or her physical, emotional, and other developmental needs. The following concepts are among those covered: greetings and departures, feeding, diapering and toileting, dressing and bathing, sleeping and naptime, health and safety. Lists of appropriate and inappropriate practices and suggested reading are also included in this guide. Janet Gonzalez-Mena, M.A., is the author.

1990, 136 pp., illus.
Item No. 0877—$12.50

Infant/Toddler Caregiving: A Guide to Setting Up Environments

This publication informs caregivers and program managers about designing settings suitable for groups of various sizes and children of different ages. Readers also learn about dividing space in family child care and child care center settings. Practical tips, suggested readings, and a glossary are also included. J. Ronald Lally, Ed.D., and Jay Stewart, M.A., coauthored the guide.

1990, 78 pp., illus.
Item No. 0879—$12.50

MODULE II: VIDEOS

It's Not Just Routine: Feeding, Diapering, and Napping Infants and Toddlers

Caregiving routines are presented from the infant's perspective. Also demonstrated are appropriate health, safety, and environmental practices for each routine. The content of the video emphasizes that such routines are opportunities for individualized, responsive caregiving that can facilitate each child's development. A 20-page video magazine is included.

1990, 24 min.

English
Item No. 0869—$65.00

Spanish
Item No. 0881—$65.00

Chinese (Cantonese)
Item No. 0882—$65.00

50 additional video magazines (in English only)
1990
Item No. 9955—$17.50

Together in Care: Meeting the Intimacy Needs of Infants and Toddlers in Groups

During infancy children need deep connections with each person who cares for them, both with their parents and with caregivers in group care settings. This video presents three child care program policies that will lead to this special kind of care: primary caregiver assignments, use of small groups, and continuity of care. A 14-page video magazine is included.

1992, 30 min.

English
Item No. 1044—$65.00

Spanish
Item No. 0888—$65.00

Chinese (Cantonese)
Item No. 1051—$65.00

50 additional video magazines (in English only)
1992
Item No. 9873—$17.50

Respectfully Yours: Magda Gerber's Approach to Professional Infant/ Toddler Care

J. Ronald Lally, Ed.D., interviews Madga Gerber, M.A., an internationally recognized leader in infant care. A variety of topics are covered, with scenes from caregiving settings illustrating points that Ms. Gerber makes during the interview. A 20-page video magazine is included.

1988, 58 min.

English
Item No. 0753—$65.00

Spanish
Item No. 0773—$65.00

Chinese (Cantonese)
Item No. 0774—$65.00

50 additional video magazines (in English only)
1988
Item No. 9958—$17.50

To place credit card orders, call, toll-free, 1-800-995-4099.

Child Development 33

Trainer's Manual: Module II, Group Care

 This new publication presents activities, handouts, transparencies, and other instructional aids that enhance the use of the program's module materials.

1993, 158 pp., loose-leaf
Item No. 1076—$20.00

MODULE II: VIDEOS

Space to Grow: Creating a Child Care Environment for Infants and Toddlers

The powerful influence of environments on infants and toddlers is described. Infants are limited in their ability to move away from an environment or to change one to their liking. The video demonstrates eight qualities for caregivers to consider when they are planning an environment for the care of infants and toddlers: health, safety, comfort, convenience, child size, flexibility, movement, and choice. A 14-page video magazine is included.

1988, 22 min.

English
Item No. 0752—$65.00

Spanish
Item No. 0775—$65.00

Chinese (Cantonese)
Item No. 0776—$65.00

50 additional video magazines (in English only)
1988
Item No. 9959—$17.50

Save by purchasing an entire module at special discount prices.

MODULE I PACKAGE — $199

Module I: Social-Emotional Growth and Socialization

Three videos with accompanying video magazines
One curriculum guide (English only)
One Trainer's Manual (English only)

If items are purchased individually, the total cost is $227.50.
The package price for Module I is $199.00.

Item No. 9928—English
Item No. 9929—Spanish
Item No. 9930—Chinese (Cantonese)

MODULE II PACKAGE — $269

Module II: Group Care

Four videos with accompanying video magazines
Two curriculum guides (English only)
One Trainer's Manual (English only)

If items are purchased individually, the total cost is $305.00.
The package price for Module II is $269.00.

Item No. 9931—English
Item No. 9932—Spanish
Item No. 9933—Chinese (Cantonese)

MODULE III PACKAGE — $159

Module III: Learning and Development

Two videos with accompanying video magazines
One curriculum guide (English only)
One Trainer's Manual (English only)

If items are purchased individually, the total cost is $175.00.
The package price for Module III is $159.00.

Item No. 9860—English
Item No. 9861—Spanish
Item No. 9862—Chinese (Cantonese)

34   Child Development

To place credit card orders, call, toll-free, 1-800-995-4099.

Learning and Development

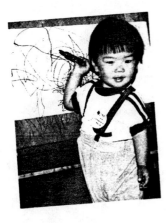

"These materials are timely and excellent for supporting the quality of child care we all want for our children."

T. Berry Brazelton, M.D.
Clinical Professor of Pediatrics
Child Development Unit
Children's Hospital Medical Center
Boston, Massachusetts

Infant/Toddler Caregiving: A Guide to Language Development and Communication

This publication emphasizes that the home language and culture of children play a vital role in their early development and care. Also included are references, caregivers' practices, warning signs, points to consider, and suggested readings for each of the topics covered in five articles.

1990, 78 pp., illus.
Item No. 0880—$12.50

Trainer's Manual: Module III, Learning and Development

NEW This easy-to-follow guide offers lesson plans, support materials, and prepared text for handouts.

Available spring, 1995.

Infant/Toddler Caregiving: A Guide to Cognitive Development and Learning

NEW The focus of this guide is exploring the contribution of responsive caregiving in relation to the naturally occurring activities of infants and toddlers to their learning and development.

Available spring, 1995.

MODULE III: VIDEOS

Ages of Infancy: Caring for Young, Mobile, and Older Infants

This video divides infancy into three different stages of development: the young, the mobile, and the older infant or toddler. Each stage is characterized by its own crucial developmental issue: for the young, security is the focus; for the mobile infant, it is exploration; for the older infant, it is the quest for identity. Specific guidelines and suggestions for caregiving are offered. A 10-page video magazine is included.

1990, 22 min.

English
Item No. 0883—$65.00

Spanish
Item No. 0884—$65.00

Chinese (Cantonese)
Item No. 0885—$65.00

50 additional video magazines (in English only)

1990
Item No. 9954—$17.50

Discoveries of Infancy: Cognitive Development and Learning

Infants begin learning through simple sensorimotor experiences and move toward figuring things out. This video explores the constant quest for knowledge of infants and toddlers. It shows six major kinds of discoveries children make in the first three years of life and offers guidelines on how to support early learning. A 14-page video magazine is included.

1992, 32 min.

English
Item No. 1045—$65.00

Spanish
Item No. 0829—$65.00

Chinese (Cantonese)
Item No. 0784—$65.00

50 additional video magazines (in English only)

1992
Item No. 9874—$17.50

Preface

At a time when half the mothers in the United States are gainfully employed, most of them full time, more young children require care outside the home than ever before. The growth of child care services has failed to keep pace with the rapidly increasing demand, making appropriate care for young children difficult for families to find. Training is needed to increase the number of quality child care programs, yet the traditional systems for training child care providers are overburdened. In response to the crisis, the California State Department of Education's Child Development Division has developed an innovative and comprehensive approach to training infant and toddler caregivers called The Program for Infant/Toddler Caregivers. The program is a comprehensive training system consisting of a document entitled *Visions for Infant/Toddler Care: Guidelines for Professional Caregiving,* an annotated guide to media training materials for caregivers, a series of training videotapes, and a series of caregiver guides.

The purpose of the caregiver guides is to offer information based on current theory, research, and practice to caregivers in both centers and family child care homes. Each guide addresses an area of infant development and care, covering major issues of concern and related practical considerations. The guides are intended to be used hand in hand with the program's series of videos; the videos illustrate key concepts and caregiving techniques for a specific area of care and the guides provide extensive and in-depth coverage of a topic.

This guide was written by Janet Gonzalez-Mena, an expert in the area of routines in infant/toddler care. Like the other guides in the series, this one is rich in practical guidelines and suggestions. The information and ideas presented in the document focus on how the daily routines of caring for infants and toddlers can become opportunities for promoting the child's learning and development as well as deepening the relationship between child and caregiver. Special attention is given to such topics as parents' concerns, the need for consistency between home and child care, and cultural diversity in child care programs.

ROBERT W. AGEE
Deputy Superintendent
Field Services Branch

ROBERT A. CERVANTES
Director
Child Development Division

JANET POOLE
Assistant Director
Child Development Division

about the author

Janet Gonzalez-Mena is an Instructor of Early Childhood Education at Napa Valley College. She has created and directed several infant/toddler programs in northern California.

In 1989 she wrote *Infants, Toddlers, and Caregivers* with Diane W. Eyer. In addition, Ms. Gonzalez-Mena has written a number of articles for *Young Children*, the journal of the National Association for the Education of Young Children. The articles include "What's Good for Babies?" and "Toddlers: What Are They Like?"

Ms. Gonzalez-Mena has also written about parenting. Her article for *Child Care Information Exchange*, "Mrs. Godzilla Takes on the Child Development Experts," argues that parents should not try to model themselves after preschool teachers. She is currently working on a book about the "Godzilla approach to parenting," emphasizing that parents need to accept and love that part of themselves which is not perfect, especially with respect to their child-rearing behavior. Ms. Gonzalez-Mena is also planning to write about cross-cultural and multicultural perspectives in early childhood education.

The author credits much of her knowledge and excitement about early child development and care to Magda Gerber. Ms. Gonzalez-Mena acknowledges that Magda Gerber's philosophy of respect for infants has strengthened her own convictions about the importance of treating each child, no matter how small, as a full human being.

acknowledgments

This publication was developed by the Center for Child and Family Studies, Far West Laboratory for Educational Research and Development, under the direction of J. Ronald Lally.

Special thanks go to Ruth T. (Toby) Gross, M.D., for her contributions to sections of this document; Peter L. Mangione, Carol Young-Holt, Sheila Signer, and Kathleen Bertolucci, for editorial assistance; and Janet Poole, Mary Smithberger, and Kathryn Swabel, Child Development Division, California State Department of Education, for their review and recommendations on content. Thanks are also extended to the members of the national and California review panels for their comments and suggestions. The national panel members were T. Berry Brazelton, Laura Dittman, Richard Fiene, Magda Gerber, Asa Hilliard, Alice Honig, Jeree Pawl, Sally Provence, Eleanor Szanton, Yolanda Torres, Bernice Weissbourd, and Donna Wittmer. The California panel members were Dorlene Clayton, Dee Cuney, Ronda Garcia, Jacquelyne Jackson, Lee McKay, Janet Nielsen, Pearlene Reese, Maria Ruiz, June Sale, Patty Siegel, and Lenore Thompson.

Introduction

Why have a whole guide on caregiving routines? How hard is it to give a baby a bottle, change a diaper, put on a sweater? The question is not how hard or easy it is to engage in caregiving but how to do it in such a way that both children and caregivers benefit from and find pleasure in the contact. What might otherwise be a chore or drudgery becomes an opportunity for interaction. A cycle can be established in which the caregiver sees the child's pleasure and satisfaction as evidence of a job well done and feels appreciated. The purpose of this guide is to help caregivers find ways to carry out routines that are enjoyable and convenient to themselves as well as good for the child.

Routines should be anything but routine except in the sense that they happen over and over. Instead of putting yourself on automatic pilot and getting the job done, you should view these special times every day as opportunities to interact with each child on a one-to-one basis. Each routine, no matter how often performed, should be a spontaneous event every time. That spontaneity will happen if you use those times to make real human contact—visual, verbal, and tactile. It will happen if you are sensitive to the child's responses and initiatives. It will happen if you are two people involved in a single task. It will not happen if you insensitively perform a procedure on a child or if you do the chore in order to get it over with.

The ideal is for the caregiver to use feeding, napping, and toileting or diapering routines as opportunities to build a close personal relationship with each child while the caregiver attends to the child's individual physical, emotional, and developmental needs. This approach is good not only for the child but also for the caregivers who are more apt to find satisfaction in caregiving routines when they pay attention to the whole child, not just to the immediate task.

Well-carried-out routines are effective far beyond the single immediate goal. Anyone can give a baby a bottle. But giving a baby a bottle only satisfies an obvious and immediate need. The *way* in which you give the bottle makes the experience a full one. If you do the task sensitively and effectively, you can satisfy the baby's needs for attention, tactile stimulation (holding and touching), interaction, and attachment. You can enhance the baby's self-esteem, feelings of security, cognitive skills, and language skills.

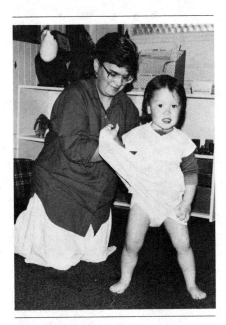

Caregivers are more apt to find satisfaction in caregiving routines when they pay attention to the whole child, not just to the immediate task.

Caregiving routines take up to 80 percent of a caregiver's time and are the basic curriculum of the infant's or toddler's day. The way in which these routines are carried out, day after day, has a major impact on young children. The caregiver's emotional tone, nonverbal messages, pace, and style of verbal communication, in addition to the actual content of the routine, need to be carefully considered.

During feeding, diapering, washing, and dressing, the child learns many things not necessarily related to the specific lesson of the routine, such as:

- Security and self-esteem
- Pleasure and tactile stimulation
- A sense of time and space as well as rhythms
- Independence and competence
- Cognitive and language skills

Routines work better in a primary caregiver system in which each caregiver has the major responsibility for specific children. This system is preferable to one in which all caregivers share equal responsibility for the whole group. If the primary caregiver is the adult who usually feeds, changes, and toilet trains the child, the two get to know each other better than if all caregivers try to concentrate on all the children. For example, sensitive and consistent napping procedures with the same caregiver, whenever possible, make it easier for children to fall asleep and offer the opportunity for intimate, personal contact.

Effective caregiving responds to each child's developmental level. Routines for *young infants (birth to nine months)* are carried out in a consistent, gentle, and timely way so that the children learn basic trust in the world. They get used to having their needs met and come to anticipate the caregiver's response to their messages.

Caregiving routines are the basic curriculum of the infant's or toddler's day.

Routines for *mobile infants (six to eighteen months)* focus on the infants' increasing competencies as the children learn to feed themselves, toddle to the sink to wash their hands, and help pull up their pants. Caregivers sensitive to this age group know that mobile infants may resist being diapered, but caregivers regard this resistance in a positive light. Instead of taking the resistance personally, the caregivers know that mobile infants would rather be moving and exploring than lying still.

Routines for *toddlers or older infants (sixteen to thirty-six months)* take into account the children's vacillation between independence and dependence. Toddlers are likely to be quite cooperative one minute, by helping to set the table, and run in the other direction the next minute when asked to hang up a coat. They may ask the caregiver to do a simple task they have been able to do for months, like putting on a shoe, then turn around and try to tie it themselves even though the task is way beyond them.

There is no formula for performing caregiving routines. They must be carried out each time as an experience shared by two people rather than a procedure one person performs on another. Caregiving is a dynamic moment-to-moment activity. Information about what and how much should be done is not memorized from books but is learned each time in the interaction with the child. For that reason this guide is just that—a guide; it is not a set of instructions or recipes on how to do caregiving routines.

This document is divided into sections on the separate caregiving routines, with practical advice on how to conduct them. Each section deals with the three age groups: the *young infant (birth to nine months)*, the *mobile infant (six to eighteen months)*, and the *toddler (sixteen to thirty-six months)*. Each section urges you to take full advantage of the opportunities each routine offers for one-to-one interactions. Each section is concerned with consistency between home and center and within the center.

The challenge for you is to take the information offered and figure out how to fit it into your own unique style of relating to infants and toddlers. How can you carry out routines in ways that are beneficial to children yet convenient and pleasurable for you? How can you do routines in ways that reflect your own personality—your unique way of dealing with the world?

Caregiving routines must be carried out each time as an experience two people share rather than a procedure one performs on the other.

Routines : Visions

Health

The caregiver promotes good health and nutrition and provides an environment that contributes to the prevention of illness.

Good health involves sound medical and dental practices through which adults model and encourage good health habits with children. Caregivers should be able to recognize common signs of illness or distress and respond promptly. Acute or chronic illness should be referred for treatment as soon as possible so that children can develop and take full advantage of the program. Children need a clean environment that is properly lighted, ventilated, and heated or cooled. Indoor and outdoor areas should be free of materials or conditions that endanger children's health. Care of the child's physical needs communicates positive feelings about his or her value and enhances the child's developing identity and sense of self-worth. Parents and caregivers should exchange information about the children's physical health frequently.

Providing *young and mobile infants* with affectionate and competent physical care includes responding to their individual rhythms while working toward regularity in feeding, sleeping, and toileting. It also includes sanitary procedures for diapering and cleaning toys that infants put in their mouths.

Toddlers imitate and learn from the activities of those around them. Good health habits can be established through modeling and encouraging toothbrushing, hand washing, eating of nutritious foods, and so on.

Nutrition

The caregiver provides a nutritious, well-balanced diet which corresponds to each infant's dietary needs and emerging eating skills, thereby fostering a positive attitude toward wholesome food and eating routines.

Good nutrition is essential to the physical, emotional, and social well-being of the developing child. Since mealtimes are an integral part of daily activities, they encompass more than just the provision of a nutritious diet. Eating should be an enjoyable experience. Mealtimes need to be relaxed and unhurried, with food served simply and attractively. Feeding activities provide not only a time for social interaction between the infant and caregiver and infant with other children but also an opportunity for learning as children experience new tastes and textures and practice their developing motor skills. Caregivers' responsibilities also include ongoing communication with parents regarding prescribed formulas, dietary requirements and restrictions, and quantities of food provided and consumed. A weekly menu should be posted to inform parents of the meals and snacks being served.

Young infants need special attention during feeding times to provide them with enough food, emotional nurturing, and cognitive stimulation for their healthy development. They thrive on familiar feeding routines with the same caregiver, when possible, and flexible schedules which allow for feedings when they are hungry. Young infants should always be held for feeding. Proper storage for mother's milk should be provided if needed; and regular milk, formula, and mother's milk should be kept refrigerated. Young infants may start to eat solid foods at about four or five months of age, beginning with smooth cereals and strained fruits and vegetables. New foods should be introduced gradually, one at a time.

Mobile infants can communicate when they want food and when they have had enough. They may be able to sit for feedings. They use their senses to explore food as they begin to feed themselves. In addition to mother's milk or formula, which still fulfills their basic nutritional needs, they can have strained fruits and vegetables and juices and also small pieces of soft foods, such as cooked carrots or sweet potatoes. Raisins, hot dogs, and other chewy foods should not be fed to mobile infants because they cannot chew well. Mobile infants may begin to drink from cups as well as bottles, and they enjoy practicing feeding themselves with a spoon while being spoon-fed. They may be very messy in their early attempts to feed themselves; but letting them handle their food helps them develop small-muscle coordination, sensory awareness, and growing feelings of autonomy.

Toddlers are ready for a wider range of solid foods as mother's milk and formula become less important sources of nutrition for them. They continue to eat cereal, fruits, and vegetables, supplementing those foods with an increasing variety of other foods. Through feeding themselves finger food and using bowls and spoons, they learn eye-hand coordination and independence. Foods which are

Caregiving Routines

The caregiver uses feeding, napping, and toileting or diapering routines as opportunities to build a close personal relationship with each child while attending to the child's physical, emotional, and developmental needs.

harder to chew can be appropriate for toddlers when the foods are cut into small pieces. Popcorn, nuts, and other hard or brittle foods, which can cause choking, are not appropriate for toddlers.

When caregivers take time to exchange eye contact, smiles, and verbal or vocal communication with young children, caregiving routines are transformed into some of the day's most interesting and pleasurable learning experiences. Feeding, napping, and diapering times are valuable learning opportunities for language, small-muscle, cognitive, and social development when children are given time to respond and participate. Young children who are fed in a relaxed, attentive way learn to enjoy their food and develop good eating habits. Having realistic expectations about children's messy eating styles can help caregivers feel comfortable about letting the children experiment and develop feeding skills. Warm and consistent napping procedures with the same caregiver whenever possible make it easier for children to fall asleep and offer the opportunity for intimate, personal contact. By moving slowly and talking in a calm way to infants and toddlers before and during diapering or toileting, caregivers can elicit cooperation and help the children develop wholesome attitudes toward their bodies and bodily functions.

Young infants learn basic trust in the world by having their physical needs attended to in a gentle and timely way. Nonmobile infants need consistency in feeding, diapering, and napping to be able to recognize and to anticipate routines, but scheduling should be flexible enough for individual needs as the children grow and change. Through responsive communication during caregiving routines, they learn the usefulness and pleasures of language.

Moblile infants explore through their senses and growing physical skills. Their competencies increase as they learn to feed themselves finger food, crawl to an eating area, or lift up a foot ready for a sock. During caregiving routines children enjoy making connections between their experiences and words that describe those experiences through spoken language or songs.

Toddlers vacillate between independence and dependence. They do, however, often appreciate the opportunity to do things for themselves. They are able to participate actively in their own feeding and enjoy getting out a diaper or a book before a nap. They may need extra time to practice skills involved in feeding or dressing themselves. Successful completion of these tasks leads to great satisfaction with themselves and the development of a healthy sense of self-esteem and competence.

These visions are excerpts from *Visions for Infant/Toddler Care: Guidelines for Professional Caregiving* (Sacramento: California Department of Education, 1988), which outlines the visions or goals of The Program for Infant/Toddler Caregivers. The Health and Nutrition statements are excerpts from Vision VI, Safety, Health, and Nutrition, and the Caregiving Routines statement is an excerpt from Vision VII, Development of Each Child's Competence.

Section One: Greetings and Departures

Arrival and departure times are important in building relationships between the caregiver and parent and between the caregiver and the child. Separation anxiety of both the parent and the child may require sensitive handling. In addition, arrival and departure times are often the only regular opportunity for exchanging information between the caregiver and parent. As the child and parent make the sometimes difficult transition from home to child care or child care to home, the caregiver and the parent exchange information and strengthen their partnership of caring for the child.

Arrival Routines

Arrivals are important because they can set the mood for the whole day. Skilled caregivers are able to greet both parent and child and make each feel welcome as well as exchange information, provide parent education, and help both cope with feelings of separation. It is quite a feat for the caregiver to attend to all those concerns in a couple of hurried minutes and still keep an eye on the other children in his or her charge. But the arrival routine can be done—and is being done on a regular basis by thousands of caregivers every day.

Information Exchange

It is important for the caregiver to learn from the parent how the child slept and ate, what mood the child is in, the state of his or her health, and family events that could influence the child. Because infants and toddlers cannot explain very well what they are experiencing, caregivers need all the pertinent information the parent has. In that way the caregiver can combine the knowledge with the child's signals in order to determine needs. Is the child crying from hunger, or is the child crying because he or she has been up since 4:30 a.m.? That is the sort of information parents can provide.

The caregiver can give the parent(s) information on what can be expected that day: "Sarah's friend Jesse is out sick today, so Sarah may feel less secure than she usually does." "Sheila is bringing her new puppies in this afternoon. Is there any problem with fears or allergies that staff should watch out for?"

Parent Education

Through this regular exchange of information, problems surface. The exchange can provide not only caregiver enlightenment but also parent education. Perhaps a mother talks about how she is at her wit's end because her child has just learned how to climb out of the crib and now she cannot get the child to sleep at night. The caregiver can describe what he or she does in the program in that case, give the parent suggestions of books to read, mention names of other parents who have recently conquered such a problem, and even invite the parent in to see how naptime is handled with children who are hard to get to sleep.

Of course the caregiver probably does not have much time to talk with the parent. The parent's time is more than likely limited, and the caregiver needs to give some attention to the child. It is quite rare that caregivers talk privately to parents during arrival time. If the child is present during the information exchange/parent education session (which is probably the case), the child should be included in the conversation in some way rather than be spoken of as though he or she were a piece of furniture. Try to give attention to both parent and child whenever possible.

Through the regular exchange of information, problems surface, giving the chance for both caregiver enlightenment and parent education.

Separation Techniques

If the child is mobile, he or she may have gone off to play while you are talking to the parent. On the other hand, the child may be hanging around, even clinging, feeling some sort of emotion about the impending good-bye. If so, you need to get through the information exchange/parent education session quickly, then try to ease both parent and child through the separation. You can do this by showing that you care about their feelings and, at the same time, showing

Help children cope with separation by:

Going slowly

Making good-bye a transition

Allowing a transition object (blanket, etc.)

Knowing what to expect from different ages

confidence that the child will be fine. Your attitude can convey a sense of security to both parent and child.

Go slowly. Do not rush the child who is dealing with feelings about the separation. In the case of young infants, the process is usually simple. You simply take the baby from the parent after he or she says good-bye. Usually, if the child is young enough, there are no tears.

If the infant or toddler is older, let him or her say good-bye and come to you—or the child can go into the play area if he or she is willing and is used to doing that. If the separation is not that easy, do not force it right away. Go into the play area, get a toy that is interesting to the child, and sit down. Offer the toy or activity in a way that says it is available but there are no strings attached. Setting the toy down slightly away from you usually gives that message. A barricade between you and the child, such as a table, may help, too. If the child is especially fearful of you, you should probably avoid contact at first, even eye contact. The mother's presence for a while, until the child gets comfortable, may help. (The video *First Moves: Welcoming a Child to a New Caregiving Setting* shows clearly how to carry out this approach.)

Making good-bye a transition instead of a sudden break can be useful unless prolonging the transition worsens it. In that case, the best solution may be for the mother simply to say good-bye and leave and allow the caregiver to deal with the child's feelings. Some children are comforted with a transitional object from home, such as a special blanket, a favorite stuffed animal, or even something of the mother's. Other children find objects in the program that comfort them; such objects should be available and offered if they help.

Knowing what to expect during various stages of development helps caregivers cope with separations. In the first months most children do not react to being left in child care. Although they react differently to their parents and to other familiar people, babies usually accept strangers. At about six months of age, infants begin to distinguish strangers and sometimes to fear them (called stranger anxiety). By nine months of age, children may be going through what is called separation anxiety and may cry lustily at even the prospect of being left in child care.

Some caregivers are surprised when the child who has been left happily for weeks suddenly starts protesting when the parent says good-bye and starts out the door. This fear of separation is a perfectly normal stage of development and shows cognitive maturation as the child comes to understand more about how the world works. Knowledge of that developmental phase may be of some comfort to the caregiver who is left with a screaming baby trying to pry the door open to follow mother or father.

The caregiver's understanding of how the parent of the fearful or protesting child may be feeling is important. The separation may be as painful for the parent as for the child. Some parents seem to suffer even more than their children. That emotion may result in ambivalent behavior as the parent feels torn between leaving and staying. If the parent has been having twinges of guilt about leaving the child, a display of separation anxiety on the part of the child may explode those twinges into overblown feelings with which the parent has trouble coping. Caregivers may need to spend time and effort comforting the parent and helping him or her move out the door. After the parent has left, further time and effort may be needed to help the child cope—although some children brighten up the minute the parent has gone.

Departure Routines

The end of the day may bring another surprising explosion of the parent's or child's feelings or both. Although many children greet their parents happily when they arrive in the afternoon, some children do not. An infant or toddler may be as matter-of-fact about mother's arrival as the child was about her departure in the morning. But that behavior may be disconcerting to the parent. If a parent is feeling a bit insecure about his or her relationship with the baby, a caregiver's well-meaning statement "He did just fine—he didn't even miss you" may tear the parent apart. The parent does not want to hear that the child suffered because of his or her absence, but the parent also does not want to hear that the child was not affected by it.

Not Wanting to Leave

Mobile infants and toddlers may be absorbed in what they are doing at the moment and may not give the attention to the parent's arrival that he or she expects. Or the child may have a particularly difficult time with transitions, with the result that he or she protests when it is time to leave. Such behavior can absolutely crush a parent. A sensitive caregiver can help the parent not to take it personally.

Then there are the children who are angry at being left in child care and who react to their parents by resisting going home at the end of the day. These children may ignore their parents or run in the other direction. Some children even cry and complain loudly. The caregiver who is not aware that this can happen may wonder at such behavior. Certainly it is surprising, but not unusual, when children who complain at being left in the morning also complain about going home in the afternoon.

Feeling Deserted

The last children to be picked up may develop feelings of being deserted. It is not unusual to see a child's anxiety mount as more and more children depart before his or her parent arrives. Reassurance as well as some special attention from the caregiver is called for here.

While dealing with feelings in both the adult and the child, the caregiver also has some physical tasks, such as turning over the diaper bag, coat, and so on. To keep the exchange simple, the caregiver should organize the child's belongings ahead of time.

Exchanging Information

The caregiver also must be aware of the parent's needs. Almost everyone is tired by the end of the day, and hunger may be another factor. Somehow, in spite of all the potential difficulties, the caregiver again must exchange information with the parent. The parent needs to

The last children to be picked up may even develop feelings of being deserted.

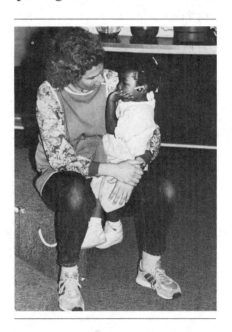

The parent needs to know what went on that day.

Arrival and departure times are important in building relationships between parent(s) and caregivers.

know what went on that day: specifics about naps, bowels, feedings, and moods. Some positive words about behavior and accomplishments are always welcome and make the parent feel more a part of the child's daily life.

If the caregiver who works the late shift does not have all this information firsthand, it is important that he or she has access to the earlier caregivers' records and shares them with the parent. The records may be a combination of checksheets with facts (times, amounts, and so on) and a log of short anecdotes.

The caregiver should end the information exchange by adding a word or two about the following day to help maintain the bond: "See you tomorrow, Jessica. The puppies will be here again, and you can pet them."

Although arrival and departure times are transitions, they are vital to building relationships between parents and caregivers. The ongoing daily contact, brief though it may be, is when the caregivers and the parents get to know each other. The caregivers learn about the parents' approaches to child rearing as well as the parents' cultures, personalities, hopes, and fears. The ideal outcome of this relationship building is a spirit of teamwork as parent and caregiver work together in partnership for the good of the child.

Points to Consider

1. How can you make the social–emotional climate during arrivals and departures warm, friendly, caring, and personal?
2. When the parents say good-bye and walk out the door, what differences in behavior might you expect from a three-month-old, a nine-month-old, and a two-year-old? How can you respond sensitively and effectively to children in each of those age groups if they are having separation difficulties?
3. How can the routines of arrival and departure be educational and therefore part of the curriculum?
4. How can arrival and departure routines be made convenient for the caregiver and meet the needs of the child and the parent?

Suggested Resources

Books and Articles

Culture and Childrearing. Edited by Ann L. Clark. Philadelphia: F. A. Davis Co., 1981.

Explores different cultural points of view on a variety of child-rearing topics, such as attachment to parents and separation.

Fraiberg, Selma H. *The Magic Years: Understanding and Handling the Problems of Early Childhood.* New York: Charles Scribner's Sons, 1984.

Offers practical information for caregivers on how to understand messages from babies and how to engage in a truly reciprocal relationship with infants.

Gonzalez-Mena, Janet, and Dianne W. Eyer. *Infants, Toddlers, and Caregivers.* Mountain View, Calif.: Mayfield Publishing Co., 1989.

Discusses how to respect children's feelings while helping them cope with situations such as separation.

Infant and Toddler Program Quality Review Instrument. Sacramento: California State Department of Education, 1988.

Provides guidelines for assessing the quality of programs for infants and toddlers.

Lally, J. R. "Feeling Good About Saying Goodbye," *Working Mother* (August, 1985), 54–56.

Presents a practical approach on how to help a child adapt to a new caregiving setting. The suggestions can apply to any situation in which a caregiver helps a child make a transition.

Lane, Mary, and Sheila Signer. *Infant/Toddler Caregiving: A Guide to Creating Partnerships with Parents.* Sacramento: California State Department of Education, 1990.

Explores issues and suggested approaches in relating to parents of infants and toddlers who are being introduced to a child care program. Examines in detail the meaning of separation for the parent as well as for the child.

Visions for Infant/Toddler Care: Guidelines for Professional Caregiving. Sacramento: California State Department of Education, 1988.

Presents goals or visions for quality care of infants and toddlers, which should be considered by caregivers and directors of child care.

Audiovisuals

Babies Are People, Too. Los Angeles: Churchill Films, 1985. Videocassette or 16 mm film, color, 27 minutes; printed guide.

Focuses on the relationship between young mothers and their children during the first two years of life. Demonstrates techniques for smoother transitions from child care at the end of the day. Available from Churchill Films, 662 North Robertson Blvd., Los Angeles, CA 90069-9990. Telephone: (213) 657-5110; (800) 334-7830.

First Moves: Welcoming a Child to a New Caregiving Setting. Child Care Video Magazine. Sacramento: California State Department of Education, 1988. Videocassette, color, 26 minutes; printed guide.

Presents practical techniques caregivers can use to introduce young children to a new care setting and ease often difficult separations between the parent and the child..

Human Development: A New Look at the Infant—Attachment (Program 5). Irvine Calif.: Concept Media, 1983. Videocassette or filmstrip/sound cassette, color, 27 minutes; printed guide.

Reviews Mary Ainsworth's work in the area of attachment. Discusses attachment behaviors and the role they play in separations and reunions. Explores the importance of caregiver sensitivity. Available from Concept Media, P.O. Box 19542, Irvine, CA 92713-9542.

Section Two: Feeding

Feeding is one of the most important activities in any infant/ toddler program. Attention to the way the caregiver feeds children in his or her care can produce a wealth of benefits.

The feeding process not only promotes physical development but may enhance cognitive and language development as well. Perhaps most important of all are the social and emotional experiences that come with feeding: feeding enhances attachment, increases feelings of security, and provides warmth, acceptance, and an overall sense of well-being.

Communicating with Children

When a familiar caregiver takes a hungry young infant in his or her arms, the message should be, "I'm here for you. I care about you. I have time for you." When the caregiver sits with an older infant, patiently feeding that child cereal, allowing the child to explore and experiment with a hand or spoon, the message is the same; in addition, the caregiver is saying, "I value your curiosity, sensory needs, and growing independence." When the caregiver sits pleasantly with a group of toddlers, helping them serve portions, talking about the food, replacing dropped spoons, and offering sponges for spills, he or she is

The more the home and the program can coordinate food and eating routines, the better.

Individual, family, and cultural perspectives on food must be discovered and taken into consideration.

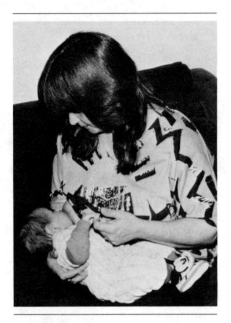

giving the message that mealtime is an important social time, that the children are increasing their self-help skills, and that the children are capable, worthy human beings who are cared about.

Communicating with Parents

Caregivers' communication with parents about the feeding process is essential. The more the home and the program can coordinate food and eating routines, the better. Caregivers need to know about the child's dietary history and needs, schedules, habits, tastes, preferences, allergies, and sensitivities; they also need to convey to parents what was offered, what was consumed, and how the child received the food that day.

Records for young infants are fairly simple because most of their nutritional needs are met through breast milk or formula. For the parent's information, daily records should be kept of how much was consumed and when, also what solids were offered and consumed. For mobile infants, a record is still necessary; these children may be trying new foods. The parents need to know when new foods are served in case the food causes digestive or behavioral reactions, which can range from diarrhea to hives to emotional upset. For toddlers, post menus of meals and snacks where parents can see the notices and keep some kind of individual record.

Individual, family, and cultural perspectives on food must be discovered and considered, even though accommodating the family's preferences may complicate the program. For example, if a child has a milk sensitivity, it is important that the child not be given milk; instead, give a substitute of which the parent approves. If the family is vegetarian, it is important that the staff respects the meat restriction and finds ways to combine foods to ensure toddlers receive complete protein. Infants get the protein they need from breast milk or formula.

If the family's cultural approaches to infant nutrition differ from mainstream approaches, the caregiver should consider feeding the child what he or she is used to, when feasible. The natural diet of most cultures is nutritionally sound, though some diets may seem strange and perhaps unbalanced. Learning about diets of other cultures can also be educational and personally interesting for caregivers.

Breast-feeding

Any mother who has an inclination to breast-feed should be encouraged to do so. The program that supports breast-feeding mothers makes a comfortable, quiet corner for them to be with their babies while feeding and minimizes interruptions. Of course, the caregivers do not make the decision but they can do a lot to encourage or discourage breast-feeding. Breast milk is designed for human infants and has exactly what they need in the proportions they need. Formula works well, but it is second best.

Although breast-feeding takes some planning and attention, many working or student mothers find they can continue to breast-feed even when the infant spends the day in another's care. The caregiver supports the practice by willingly accepting bottles of breast milk and by allowing, even encouraging, the mother to drop by for feedings (even though this may inconvenience the staff, who might find feeding the child formula easier than waiting until the mother can come in).

Bottle-feeding

Most young infants will be bottle-fed by caregivers, whether the bottles contain breast milk or formula. (The formula should be similar to what they get at home.) Even though bottle-fed, infants should receive the same personalized attention as the baby who is breast-fed by his or her own mother. Babies should be held for bottle-feeding. Focused attention by a primary caregiver ensures that all babies will get both the right amount of food and emotional nurturing.

The feeding schedule should be individualized for each infant and flexible enough to accommodate the child's daily needs. Infants should be fed when hungry, not when the clock or schedule dictates. Consistent care is important in feeding young infants. They need to come to expect that, soon after they communicate hunger, they will be fed by a familiar caregiver who understands their signals and is in tune with them.

What does it mean to be an "in-tune" caregiver? In-tune caregivers read the baby's signals and respond appropriately. They are sensitive. For example, when feeding a very young infant, caregivers soon realize that the baby cannot look and suck at the same time or listen and look and suck. In-tune caregivers are careful not to distract or entertain when the baby is hungrily eating, yet they are willing to play briefly when the baby stops for a short time, after taking the edge off his or her hunger, and indicates an interest in the adult. In-tune caregivers know when to burp the baby, and they stop the feeding when the baby indicates he or she has had enough. Sensitive caregivers know each baby's individual quirks—what nipple works best for that baby, for example. The video *Getting in Tune: Creating Nurturing Relationships with Infants and Toddlers* explains this concept of reading signals and responding appropriately.

The mobile infant continues to need the focused attention of a primary caregiver when the infant is being bottle-fed. Even though the mobile infant is capable of holding the bottle and moving and drinking at the same time, he or she needs to be held in a caregiver's arms during the bottle-feeding.

The child who arrives in the program used to treating a bottle as a pacifier to carry around and play with may protest not being allowed to do so, but the caregiver who values feeding as a time of nutrition as

Babies should be held for bottle-feeding and fed when hungry.

well as closeness, not as simple oral gratification, will persist despite protests. Of course, the bottle takes on less nutritional importance as the child grows older and begins drinking from a cup and eating solid foods.

Weaning

When a child can meet all his or her nutritional needs from eating solid food and is able to drink satisfactorily from a cup, the child may be weaned from the bottle or breast. However, weaning at that time may not always be appropriate, depending on the inclinations of the parent or the baby or both. Ideas about and approaches to weaning are as strong and varied as those on starting solid food. Two approaches are described here.

Weaning can begin early on as a very gradual process by giving liquids other than formula or breast milk from a spoon, starting from the first weeks. As the child matures, a cup is introduced long before the child can hold it independently; he or she learns to drink with the adult holding the cup. As the child becomes a proficient drinker while holding the cup, the daily number of bottles or breast-feeding sessions is decreased gradually until he or she takes all liquids from a cup and no longer takes the bottle or breast. Some people who use this approach aim to complete the weaning process about the end of the first year—when the infant no longer needs the bottle for nutrition and may become emotionally attached to it if the bottle is continued.

Another approach to weaning is not to worry about it or even plan for it but to let the child determine when to give up the bottle or breast. The cup is introduced at an appropriate age, but no attempt is made to cut down on bottles or breast-feedings. If the adult does not become impatient, the child "outgrows" the need, although the age at which this happens can vary greatly—from one year to as late as six years. In some cultures, breast-feeding a six-year-old is not shocking.

More commonly, however, sometime before the second or third birthday, parents decide they have had enough of bottles or breast-feeding and stop. Usually that happens without too much trouble unless the child has a strong emotional attachment or the issue becomes a power struggle.

Go by what the parent wants, within reason, both in introducing solids and in weaning. You may have strong opinions, too, but they may not coincide with those of the parent. Be respectful of the parent's preferences, and when there is a critical difference of viewpoint or opinion, discussion and negotiation with a parent are always in order.

Starting Solid Foods

Currently recommended practice suggests four to six months of age is the right time to start solid foods. According to Mike Samuels and

Ideas about and approaches to weaning are as strong and varied as those on starting solid food.

Discussion and negotiation with a parent are always in order when there is a difference of viewpoint or opinion.

Nancy Samuels in *The Well Baby Book,* before that time, "studies of stool samples show that most of the food passes through undigested. The young baby is not able to break down the complex molecules in many fats, carbohydrates, and protein."[1] However, some parents have very different ideas about introducing solids, ranging from wanting to start at a few weeks (the claim is the child sleeps better because the stomach stays full longer) to waiting a year. The reasons range from personal to cultural.

When introducing a new food to infants and toddlers, take individual temperaments into consideration. Some children will take delight in each new experience whether it is food or a new toy. Those children relish novelty. Other children will be much more cautious about something new, and you need to go more slowly with such children. They are likely to spit out the first taste of a new food. Do not force them but keep trying. Be patient. Repeated exposure over a period of time is the key to success with the cautious child. The temperaments of infants and toddlers are important considerations in carrying out routines. The video *Flexible, Fearful, or Feisty: The Different Temperaments of Infants and Toddlers* presents more information about temperament and offers suggestions for caregiving.

Infants

Infants should be introduced to new foods gradually, one food at a time. For example, you may offer one taste the first day, a spoonful the second day, two spoonfuls the third day. Take a week before giving a full serving. That way the child slowly gets used to the new flavor and texture, and if he or she is sensitive, you will know to which food so you can stop before triggering a strong reaction.

Keep beginner foods simple. Do not add sugar, salt, or spices—infants appreciate the natural flavors of food without the additives

Infants should be introduced to new foods gradually, one food at a time.

An in-tune caregiver reads the baby's signals and responds appropriately.

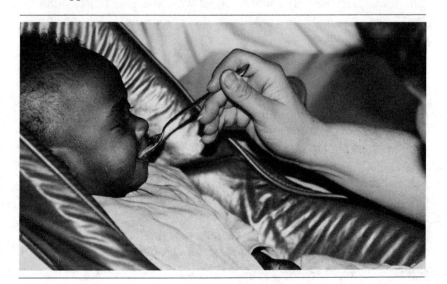

most adults are so used to. Avoid processed foods with artificial flavors or colors. It does not make sense to add complicated chemicals to a young system. Cereal, particularly infant rice cereal, is the most common food to start with. Moistened with formula or breast milk, the cereal can be as pasty or runny as you find effective for easy spoon-feeding.

Be sure you are thoroughly acquainted with the parents' plan for introducing new foods. Try to be as consistent with the home as possible. If the parents or their pediatrician have a particular order for new food introduction, respect it. Some parents and pediatricians believe that if you introduce sweet foods such as strained fruits first, the child will resist strained vegetables and meat. Other parents and pediatricians believe that the best method is to introduce fruits first because the sweetness is familiar to the child.

Most pediatricians advise delaying the introduction of certain foods that infants are commonly allergic to, such as egg white, orange juice, wheat products, and chocolate. Of course, infants should not be fed fried or greasy foods of any sort.

Be careful that the child can manage finger foods and will not choke.

Introduce strained foods first and finger foods later, being careful that the child can manage the finger foods and will not choke on them. Anything with a hard or crunchy texture that can be bitten off but is difficult to chew is inappropriate for the young and the mobile infant. Avoid carrot sticks and apple slices, especially with peels. Even some soft foods can be dangerous. For example, hot dogs, hot dog rounds, marshmallows, peanut butter, and grapes have all been known to cause choking.

Know each child's ability to swallow. Sometimes children with slight, even undetected neurological problems cannot coordinate chewing, swallowing, and breathing and will gag or choke easily. Often parents can tell you whether their children need special attention in this area. Be very cautious about what you give those children to eat, even when they are toddlers and everyone else is having an easy time with the food.

Toddlers

Older mobile infants and toddlers, who are no longer strictly dependent on breast milk or formula for nutrition, need a wider variety of foods—both those eaten with utensils and finger foods. However, even toddlers should be restricted from foods such as popcorn, peanuts and other nuts, peanut butter, hot dogs, hot dog rounds, and grapes because of the danger of choking. And toddlers with any history of or inclination toward swallowing difficulties should be restricted to the soft, safe foods of infants.

When you introduce a new food, take a positive attitude, as if you expect each child will like the food. If not all do, do not react too strongly. You can suggest matter-of-factly that each child taste the new food, but do not insist that it be eaten. Also, do not get into a power struggle over the one taste. Toddlers are known to change their minds easily; if you do not make a fuss, the chances are the children will not do so either the next time the food appears. They will probably try it and may even like it.

Older toddlers may serve themselves and be encouraged not to take more than they can eat.

The foods you serve toddlers should reflect their cultures and accommodate their personal tastes as far as possible. Toddlers, like infants, need no additives in their foods—even additives such as salt, sugar, spices, or artificial colors or flavors. However, the children may have acquired a taste for the flavor of the table food they are served at home, so trying to keep the children's food pure, simple, and natural may be difficult and may be in conflict with family or cultural tastes.

Offer children a balanced diet, but let them determine what and how much they will eat. If you offer a range of nutritious foods (fruits, vegetables, whole grains in the form of cereals and breads, legumes such as peas and beans, dairy products, eggs, and meat), children will, over a period of time, select for themselves a balanced diet even though they may make unbalanced choices on any given day. Your responsibility ends at offering a balance of foods and feeding children unable to feed themselves. It is not your responsibility to force children to eat certain foods or amounts of foods.

Do not spoon-feed children who can feed themselves. Do not scold or punish children for what they eat or do not eat. (When you do that, you get out of tune with the child, as the video *Getting in Tune: Creating Nurturing Relationships with Infants and Toddlers* shows.) Give small enough servings so that children can ask for seconds, thus stimulating appetites and minimizing waste. Older toddlers may serve themselves and be encouraged not to take more than they can eat.

Feeding schedules may be less individualized for older mobile infants and toddlers, who can wait a bit longer than the young infant when hungry. You should continue to pay attention to individual needs, but you can also take group needs into consideration. Toddlers can eventually learn to eat as a group on a regular schedule that includes mealtimes and scheduled snacks. However, provision should still be made for the child who is hungry at unscheduled periods or who arrives unfed just after breakfast has been cleared away.

Use of a Spoon

Capitalize on children's interest in feeding themselves from the first time the infant grabs the spoon. (Get another spoon when that happens and work as a team, letting the child explore and experiment with self-feeding.) Do not worry about the mess. Infants need to handle food in order to build coordination and develop their ability to feed themselves. Infants also derive valuable sensory experiences by being allowed to touch the food at a young age. The children's growing feelings of autonomy are worth the effort it takes to clean up the mess. Do stop the activity when it no longer has an eating focus. When the child has had enough to eat, it is better to remove the food than to turn it into a plaything.

Be aware of the strong feelings some parents or staff members may have about infants "playing" with food even when you realize that the children are building self-feeding skills and having valuable exploration experiences. For example:

- Some cultures have strong prohibitions against doing anything with food besides eating it.
- Some parents see food on hands as a waste of a precious commodity.

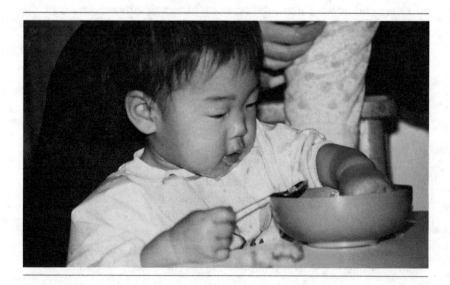

Infants need the freedom to touch and handle their food.

- Some parents cannot stand to see their children smeary and gooey, even temporarily.
- Some cultures spoon-feed children right up to five or six years of age, preferring that they not feed themselves until they can do it neatly, with skill and manners. Respect the parents' differing goals and value systems.

Socializing at Mealtimes

In the past, many families shared mealtimes as a daily social occasion. In some homes that custom is still true today, but families who spend most of the day apart have difficulty scheduling mealtimes together. Therefore, sociable mealtimes are important for infants and toddlers in child care.

A few general principles about social mealtimes apply to all age levels:

- The atmosphere should be calm and pleasant.
- The environment should be appropriate and attractive.
- Adults should participate in mealtimes with children.
- Conversation should be part of the eating experience.
- Children should eat when they are hungry.
- Children should not have to wait for food.
- Children should be free to leave the eating area when they have finished eating and have been cleaned up.

Infants

When young infants are bottle-fed, they should be in the arms of a familiar caregiver in as secluded a place as possible, where they are not distracted by excess noise and activity. The adult should be calm and relaxed, able to focus the fullest possible attention on the child being fed. How much or little the adult talks, hums, or sings during the feeding process depends on the individual child and whether the adult's actions add to the experience. No hungry young infant should have to wait very long to be fed. Infants should not be left crying from hunger but should be fed soon after the crying starts. Stop feeding an infant when he or she indicates fullness, not when the bottle or bowl is empty.

Stop feeding an infant when he or she indicates fullness, not when the bottle or bowl is empty.

Mobile infants should be seated comfortably when solids are being fed. Infants should not be left waiting, strapped in a row of high chairs, while the food is being prepared and other babies are being fed. Nor should children be left in the high chairs when they have finished eating, even though the adult does not consider the mealtime over. A calm, relaxed, attentive, conversational adult should be part of the process.

Mobile infants can be fed in small groups seated at tables in appropriately sized chairs. The children's feet should touch the ground.

Mobile infants can be fed at tables. Their feet should touch the ground.

(See the video *Space to Grow: Creating a Child Care Environment for Infants and Toddlers* for more information about child-sized equipment.) A little guidance may be needed to teach children to remain at the table while eating. You can provide this guidance by taking the food from children who leave the table with it and telling them that leaving the table means they have finished. You can give the children a warning, bring them back once, and from then on enforce the rule by not allowing children back to the table once they make the decision to leave.

Some programs prefer to use high chairs for mobile infants. If you choose to use high chairs, be especially sensitive not to keep children waiting in them before or after eating.

Toddlers

Toddlers usually eat in groups at tables and enjoy helping to set the table and serve themselves. The smaller the group, the less hectic the meal. An adult should be seated with each group. When the adult eats along with the children, he or she is able to model attitudes, manners, and skills, which is the most effective way to teach. By the time children are toddlers, the give-and-take interactions of earlier months have become real mealtime conversations about the food, the events of the day, the events to come, news from home, and so on.

Washing Up

The last step in the process of feeding infants and toddlers is cleanup. For the young infant who takes only a bottle, the step is very simple and involves rinsing or washing the bottle and nipple. The child often remains clean unless the infant has spit up. A cloth is usually kept close at hand for that purpose.

Toddlers can help set up and clean up.

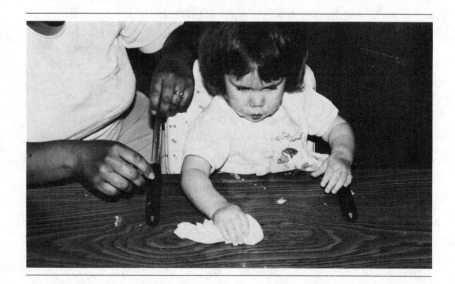

Mobile infants at the end of a meal may be quite a different story, depending on what they have been eating and whether they have been helping to feed themselves. Use a clean washcloth to wash each child's hands and face, involving the child as much as possible in the washing up process. Bibs will protect clothes, but now and then a change of clothes may be in order after a particularly messy meal.

Toddlers can help clean up—both themselves and the table. If an empty dishpan is available, toddlers can dispose of their own dirty dishes, sponge their own place at the table, and go to a low sink and wash their own hands and face with a little help. Of course, some days toddlers feel more independent than other days, which will determine how much you need to urge or help them to do the cleanup.

Helping the Finicky Eater

Although most children enjoy eating, differences in taste, appetite, and history of eating may make some children very fussy eaters. The following examples show why some children became fussy eaters.

Normal Appetite Decrease

As an infant Jane had no problem eating. She enjoyed her bottle, and when solids were introduced, she enjoyed them as well. Her mother was used to Jane's eating everything offered. Then about the age of two, Jane's appetite suddenly decreased and her temper increased. Her mother worried because instead of eating the good-sized meals she used to eat, Jane started shoving her almost full plate away, saying "s'nuff!"

Jane's mother did not understand that a dramatic decrease in appetite after the first two years—when the growth rate slows down—is normal. Babies eat so much because they grow so fast;

weight gains can be charted on a daily basis for the first months. By two years of age that is no longer the case.

Jane's mother, used to the infant's large food intake and rapid growth, worried about her child. She tried to get Jane to eat more. She tried feeding the child, playing games with her, urging her to eat. All the mother did was trigger angry responses. Before long, eating became a big issue, and mother and child were locked in a power struggle.

When Jane arrived in child care, she brought her eating history with her and immediately established a reputation as a fussy eater. She barely ate anything, and although staff did not worry, her mother did—a great deal. Jane and her food intake were the subject of many parent-caregiver conferences, both formal and informal, until the staff finally convinced the mother to relax and stop making an issue of eating. Jane is still a light eater but she is making normal weight gains, and now no one is worried about her.

Complications of Prematurity

Mike was born prematurely and stayed in the hospital for three months, during which time he encountered a number of life-threatening complications and illnesses. He was fed through a tube directly into his stomach most of those three months. Learning to suck a nipple while he was coordinating breathing and swallowing was not easy for Mike.

When he came home from the hospital, Mike spent most of his time sleeping and had to be awakened to be fed. He often fell asleep before he had consumed more than an ounce or two. Then he suffered a severe case of diarrhea and became dehydrated, which put him back in the hospital.

Mike's mother was told how important it was that she get a certain amount of food and fluids into Mike and that it was her fault that he was dehydrated. From then on she took a vigorous approach to feeding her son—insisting that he finish his bottles. When he started eating solid foods, she pushed him to eat although he showed little interest.

When Mike entered child care, he was a healthy fifteen-month-old, a little thin but not abnormally so. Although he enjoyed his bottle, he did not like solid foods very much. Mike's mother and the staff together explored ways to improve his enjoyment of solids, discovering what flavors and textures most appealed to him. They found that Mike liked finger food best and tried to find ways to give him a greater variety of foods he could pick up himself, even though the other babies were eating food that mostly required bowls and spoons.

Unhealthy Eating Habits

Brian was always a big eater. He consumed volumes of food but only the kinds to which he was accustomed. Some of the people in his home lived on doughnuts, chips, cola, sugar-coated cereal, and fast foods—and Brian quickly developed a taste for the family diet. He turned up his nose at the food in the center, which consisted of fresh fruit, cooked and fresh vegetables, meat, fish, whole grain bread, and cereals (without sugar coatings). He went all day without eating and then stuffed himself with the snacks available at home in the evening.

Worried both that he was overweight and about his eating habits, Brian's mother talked to the staff about what to do. Together they formed a plan to continue offering him the natural wholesome food served at the center and to cut down on the junk food available at home. When Brian could no longer consume the large number of empty calories at home in the evening, his daytime appetite increased and he began to eat selectively from the food served at the center. He still does not eat the balanced diet the staff would prefer, but both his eating habits and his weight have improved.

General Guidelines

Although each finicky eater has a separate story and needs to be considered individually, there are some general approaches to adopt:

- Try to understand the origin of the problem.
- Work closely with the parent both to understand the problem and to look for solutions.
- If the child is gaining weight normally, do not worry about the amount consumed.
- Offer only nourishing food in attractive and *small* servings.
- Stay out of power struggles. One way to do that is to give some choices.
- Take as much of the negative emotional tone out of mealtimes as possible.
- See if altering the environment in which the food is presented makes a difference. For example, does the child eat better when the meal is a "picnic" outside? Does the child eat better alone?

Information about feeding needs to pass freely between caregiver and parent on a regular basis. The knowledge makes a difference to the caregiver if an infant arrives without having eaten. How else is the caregiver to know, when the baby cries, whether the cry is from hunger or for some other reason? At the end of the day, the parent of a toddler needs to know when the child last ate and how much, in order to plan dinner.

The information can be exchanged informally when parents and primary caregivers see each other regularly at the beginning and end of the day. However, changing shifts may get in the way of that informal communication system, in which case a written system is called for. Some centers have chalkboards to record the information daily. Others have forms to fill out for each child. Still others keep the information in notebooks available to parents. However the record-keeping is done, the flow of information is vital to the caregiver's and the parent's job as well as to each child's well-being.

Points to Consider

1. How well do your feeding routines reflect your program's philosophy? Look for examples of the ways in which you carry out your goals through your approaches to feeding. Consider goals of health and safety as well as of physical, social, emotional, and cognitive development. Is increasing independence one of your goals? Do your feeding routines promote that goal?

2. What ways have you found to balance the feeding needs of infants and toddlers with your own convenience and comfort?

3. How consistent are the feeding routines in your program? Are the routines full of daily surprises for the children, or can the children learn to predict what will happen and thus add to their sense of security?

4. How well do your feeding routines for each child match those of his or her home? Do you have continual communication with parents in order to provide as much consistency as possible between home and day care?

5. Does each child get individual attention during feeding routines? Are the routines set up in such a way that you have the opportunity for one-on-one interactions?

Note

1. Mike Samuels and Nancy Samuels, *The Well Baby Book*. New York: Summit Books, 1979, p. 147.

Suggested Resources

Books and Articles

Brazelton, T. Berry. *Infants and Mothers: Differences in Development*. New York: Delacorte Press, 1983.

Describes how temperamental differences influence the lives and care of infants.

Gerber, Magda. "Caring for Infants with Respect: The RIE Approach," *Zero to Three* (February, 1984), 1–3.

Presents Magda Gerber's approach to caring for infants and toddlers: she recommends that caregivers always respect babies.

Gonzalez-Mena, Janet, and Dianne W. Eyer. *Infants, Toddlers, and Caregivers*. Mountain View, Calif.: Mayfield Publishing Co., 1989.

Discusses feeding infants and toddlers as part of the caregiving routines that make up a major part of the child care curriculum.

Infant and Toddler Program Quality Review Instrument. Sacramento: California State Department of Education, 1988.

Provides guidelines for assessing the quality of programs for infants and toddlers.

Leach, Penelope. *Your Baby and Child: From Birth to Age Five*. New York: Alfred A. Knopf, Inc., 1978.

Offers practical, useful advice about the care of babies.

A Manual for Parents and Professionals. Edited by Magda Gerber. Los Angeles: Resources for Infant Educarers, 1978.

Explains how the RIE method works and gives practical advice about how to put respect into caregiving routines, such as feeding. Available from Resources for Infant Educarers (RIE), 1550 Murray Circle, Los Angeles, CA 90026.

Samuels, Mike, and Nancy Samuels. *The Well Baby Book*. New York: Summit Books, 1979.

Examines babies' needs and health issues from a holistic health perspective.

Nash, M., and C. Tate. "Nutrition and Feeding," in *Better Baby Care: A Book for Family Day Care Providers*. Washington, D.C.: The Children's Foundation, 1986, pp. 79–84.

Provides information about how to feed infants and toddlers. Although written for family child care providers, the information will be useful to center caregivers as well.

Spock, Benjamin M., and Michael Rothenberg. *Dr. Spock's Baby and Child Care: Fortieth Anniversary Edition*. New York: E.P. Dutton, 1985.

An update of Dr. Spock's classic, the book has useful advice on the care of infants and toddlers.

Thoman, Evelyn B., and Sue Browder. *Born Dancing: The Relaxed Parents' Guide to Making Babies Smart with Love*. New York: Harper and Row Pubs., Inc., 1987.

Explores how babies communicate and describes how caregivers can trust, respect, and understand babies' unspoken language and natural rhythms, thus engaging in a dance with the infants.

Visions for Infant/Toddler Care: Guidelines for Professional Caregiving. Sacramento: California State Department of Education, 1988.

Presents goals or visions for quality care of infants and toddlers, which should be considered by caregivers and directors of child care.

Audiovisuals

Day Care: A Comprehensive Look—Infants and Toddlers (Part I). Tuckahoe, N.Y.: Campus Films Distributors Corp., 1979. Filmstrip, color, 90 slides; sound on cassette; printed guide.

Discusses the importance of attending to the total development of the child. Emphasizes the importance of daily routines as a time for children to learn and acquire good feelings about the world. Approximately ten slides show how feeding can be enjoyable for both child and caregiver. Available from Campus Films Distributors Corp., 24 Depot Sq., Tuckahoe, NY 10707.

Day to Day with Your Child (Program 2): *The Infant's Communication.* Mount Kisco, N.Y.: Guidance Associates, 1977. Filmstrip, color, 34 minutes total (five programs); printed guide.

Deals with the importance of learning and responding to a baby's signals so the baby can develop trust and become self-reliant. Discusses feeding as a good time to talk with babies and comment on what you are doing. Available from Guidance Associates, Communications Park, Box 3000, Mount Kisco, NY 10549. Telephone: (914) 666-4100; (800) 431-1242.

Feeding Skills: Your Baby's Early Years. Los Angeles: Churchill Films, 1981. Videocassette and film, color, 24 1/2 minutes.

Gives information on helping children from age two weeks to two years to acquire eating skills; discusses the importance of feeding times to the baby's development of trust. Includes information on nutrition and food preparation. Available from Churchill Films, 662 North Robertson Blvd., Los Angeles, CA 90069-9990. Telephone: (213) 657-5110; (800) 334-7830.

Flexible, Fearful, or Feisty: The Different Temperaments of Infants and Toddlers. Sacramento: California State Department of Education, 1990. Videocassette, color, 29 minutes; printed guide.

Identifies nine temperamental traits exhibited by infants and toddlers that are typically grouped into three temperamental types, described in the video as flexible, fearful, and feisty. Provides caregivers with techniques for dealing with the differences between individual infants and toddlers in group child care settings.

Getting in Tune: Creating Nurturing Relationships with Infants and Toddlers. Child Care Video Magazine. Sacramento: California State Department of Education, 1988. Videocassette, color, 24 minutes; printed guide.

Presents the "responsive process," which includes three steps: watching, asking, and adapting. Helps the caregiver learn what a young child needs and how best to respond to that need.

It's Not Just Routine: Feeding, Diapering, and Napping Infants and Toddlers, Sacramento: California State Department of Education, 1990. Videocassette, color, 24 minutes; printed guide.

Demonstrates how to carry out feeding/eating routines with infants and toddlers. Particular attention is given to the setting, safety and health issues, and the quality of the experience for the child and the caregiver.

Menu Planning for Child Care Programs. Ithaca, N.Y.: Cornell University AV Center-C, 1973. Color, 72 slides; sound on cassette; printed text.

Shows how to plan nutritious, economical meals and snacks for groups of children in child care centers or homes. Discusses family-style serving and finger foods. Includes suggestions for toddlers. Available from Cornell University AV Center-C, 8 Research Park, Ithaca, NY 14850.

Space to Grow: Creating a Child Care Environment for Infants and Toddlers. Sacramento: California State Department of Education, 1988. Videocassette, color, 22 minutes; printed guide

Presents concepts to consider in setting up feeding and eating areas for infants and toddlers.

Section Three: Diapering and Toileting

When an adult has more than one infant or toddler to care for, the adult's attention must be divided. Some children tend to draw more attention than others. Some manage to do so because of their cuteness, others because of their difficult behavior, still others because of their ability to engage adults directly. In every group of infants and toddlers, there are some children who do not command attention. They may be the "easy-going" babies or the "cautious" babies, or they may have some other temperamental style that attracts less attention. All babies in child care, whether they demand it or not, need regular, focused attention from an adult—preferably the same adult each time. Diapering is a built-in opportunity for that attention to occur.

Diapering—A Social and Educational Activity

Perhaps the least favorite of the caregiving routines for many adults (though not necessarily for children), diapering nevertheless offers thousands of opportunities for focused, one-to-one interactions. When used to their fullest, those many diaperings enhance social development and become educational experiences as well. Diapering can become a valuable activity instead of a chore.

The child being diapered must have the caregiver's focused attention.

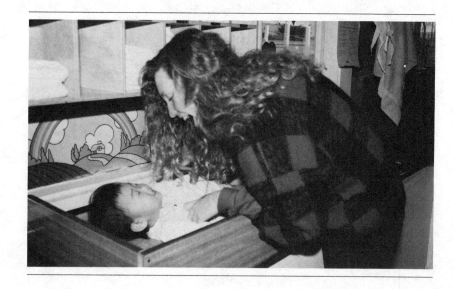

Three principles turn diapering into a constructive experience for the child:

1. The attention of the caregiver should be focused on the child and the task at hand.
2. The caregiver should treat the child with respect.
3. Talking with the child should be part of the experience.

Focused Attention

When a caregiver is responsible for several children or shares responsibility with other caregivers for a group of children, it is very difficult to give only one child focused attention—yet that is what must happen during diapering. If a team of caregivers in a program shares responsibility for a group of children, everyone on the team needs to agree that focused attention is important. Other caregivers present must be willing to take over for the caregiver diapering the child. In programs where this system works, one caregiver can focus on the baby being diapered and remain assured that the group is in good hands. While giving the child being diapered focused attention, the caregiver remains aware of the rest of the group in case the other caregivers should need additional help with a sudden problem.

When a caregiver is alone with several babies, as is usually the case in family child care, focused attention is more difficult. The caregiver can still give close attention to the baby being diapered if the environment has been set up so that it is entirely safe for every baby in it. Babies can play on their own while the caregiver's attention is on diapering. Of course, the caregiver in these circumstances will still keep an eye out for what is going on elsewhere—even if only the corner of an eye. Experienced caregivers get very good at that kind of dual attention. They can focus directly on one child while they are still aware of the several other children in their charge.

Respectful Diapering

In a respectful diapering sequence, the caregiver approaches the baby slowly, making sure that he or she is in the baby's line of vision and that the baby is not surprised at the approach. The caregiver takes time to see where the baby's attention is focused. If the baby is involved with a toy or with another baby, the caregiver does not interrupt the child right away. Instead the baby is given time to become used to the caregiver's presence. After the baby has had enough time to take notice of the caregiver, the caregiver announces that he or she is going to change the baby's diaper and gives the child time to respond. Holding out his or her arms, the caregiver then announces that he or she is going to pick up the baby—and again allows time for a response. When the baby seems to understand what is to happen (depending on the age), the caregiver picks up and carries the infant to the diapering counter.

Diapering with respect includes attending to the whole infant or toddler.

The procedure may be drawn out into a lengthy transition or it may happen quite rapidly. The point is to get the baby to focus on what will happen without feeling interrupted or distracted. The video *Respectfully Yours: Magda Gerber's Approach to Professional Infant/Toddler Care* further explains the concept of respect.

At the diapering counter, the caregiver continues to announce what will happen before it does, giving the baby a chance to take in the information. ("First I'm going to undo your overalls.") The caregiver asks for the baby's cooperation, whenever possible, involving the infant in the process. ("Please lift up your bottom for me.") The caregiver helps the child focus both on the process itself and on the child's own body and its sensations. ("That's wet, isn't it? But the water's nice and warm—feel how warm it is.")

The conversation centers on what is happening then and there. If the baby wants to play—blowing bubbles at the caregiver, for example—the caregiver responds, joining in the game and pausing in the diapering process. Then, when appropriate, the caregiver brings the baby's attention back to the task at hand.

If you think of doing something with the baby rather than doing something to the baby, you will see the difference between a respectful diapering and one that is not.

If you think of doing something *with* the baby rather than doing something *to* the baby, you will see the difference between a respectful diapering and one that is not. The message to the child from respectful diapering is: "I care about you; nothing about you disgusts me. This is a task we must work on together to get done; we can both enjoy it while we are doing it. You can learn something about yourself, the world, and me by paying attention to what is happening, and I will help you pay attention."

Object-oriented Diapering

In contrast to the respectful way of diapering is the object-oriented way. In this procedure, the infant is snatched up in the middle of whatever he or she is doing and plopped on the diapering counter with no explanation. The infant is handed a toy to play with. From then on the infant's upper half is ignored while the bottom half gets cursory attention from a caregiver who, with a frown and a wrinkled nose, cleans the child while carrying on a conversation with someone else. The child gets a very different message from that kind of diapering.

The irony is that the object-oriented way is not necessarily faster and more efficient than the respectful way, even with all the waiting that may be required by being respectful. An experienced caregiver knows that only at certain stages do babies take diapering lying down. As soon as babies can turn over, they realize they have a choice in the matter, and they may spend as much energy trying to get off the diapering counter as the caregiver does keeping them on and getting them changed. So if the caregiver is working for fast, efficient diapering, he or she is better off being respectful and trying for cooperation rather than dealing in other, less respectful ways that can easily lead to a struggle with the child.

The Older Infant's Diapering

By the end of the mobile infant stage, most infants go back to their earlier, more willing selves. As infants get older, they can be truly helpful, holding still when necessary, putting feet into pant legs, raising bottoms, and holding them up while the caregiver slides the diaper underneath. By that age the infants who have been involved in the diapering process as active participants can be distinguished from those who have been treated as passive recipients of a service performed on them.

Of course, a diapering process that does not take the individual caregiver's style into consideration is not worth much. However, once caregivers incorporate the *spirit* of respect into their systems, carrying out respectful diaperings in individual styles is not difficult.

A Convenient Environment

Adult convenience is another important consideration in the diapering process. The secret to success is in arranging the environment. All diapering supplies should be at hand. The diapering area should be near a source of warm water. Provisions for used diapers should be within reach. You should never have to leave the diapering area during a diapering. (If you do, take the baby with you—never leave a baby unattended on a diapering counter.)

Convenience requires preparation and organization. Nothing is worse than reaching for a diaper and finding the cupboard empty or wanting a clean pair of overalls and discovering they are in the diaper bag in the child's cubby. Planning ahead is vital to a smooth diapering process. The video *Space to Grow: Creating a Child Care Environment for Infants and Toddlers* has an excellent example of a convenient diapering arrangement.

You should never have to leave the diapering area during a diapering.

35

Sanitation procedures are essential in the diapering process. You should develop procedures that satisfy licensing and health requirements and post them in every diapering area. Above all, you should always follow the procedures. A sample set of procedures follows:

1. Check to be sure the diaper area has been sanitized since the last diapering. If not, discard used paper, spray with a bleach solution, and put clean paper down.
2. Wash hands before changing a diaper.
3. Dispose of used diapers in the container provided.
4. Wipe the child with a clean, moist cloth or baby wipe and put a clean diaper on the child. Dispose of the used cloth or wipe in the container provided.
5. Wash the child's hands.
6. Clean and sanitize the diapering area: discard used paper in the container provided, spray with a bleach solution, wipe with a paper towel, discard the paper towel, and put down a clean paper.
7. Wash hands thoroughly.

Toileting—Readiness in Three Developmental Areas

Toilet training or learning starts in infancy when babies are treated as partners in their diaperings. As infants become toddlers, they become more and more aware of their bodily functions and eventually begin to learn to control them. Toilet training, a natural outgrowth of this long, slow process, occurs when the child achieves readiness in three areas: physical, cognitive, and emotional.

Physical Readiness

Physical readiness for toilet learning is not enough— cognitive and emotional readiness are also necessary.

A clue to approaching physical readiness is when a toddler announces either proudly or matter-of-factly *after* urinating or defecating, "Me go peepee (poopoo)!" It is important for the caregiver to respond positively to such an announcement. It is also important for the caregiver to know what words the child uses for bodily functions in order to understand such a noteworthy announcement. Find out from the parents when they enroll their child—do not take a chance on misunderstanding.

A further clue to approaching readiness is when the child stays dry for several hours at a time. That means the bladder can hold more and for longer, a necessary prerequisite for success in using the toilet. Holding on is an important physical step. Letting go is another one. Success in using the toilet means that the child not only must hold on until he or she is bare-bottomed and actually on the toilet but also must be able to relax the sphincter muscles that close the bladder or rectum.

That kind of fine-tuned control takes much longer in some children than in others. Using the toilet is a more complicated process than it seems to those of us who learned it long ago and do not even think about it. For the beginner, the process is a different matter entirely.

Another sign of physical readiness is when the child can handle his or her own clothing, as long as the process does not involve complicated unbuttoning or untying. When signs of physical readiness appear, children should be dressed in simple clothes rather than the cute little overalls and one-piece jumpsuits that work so well with younger infants. Pants with elastic waistbands are easiest for toddlers to handle—both boys and girls. Of course, a parent who has just invested in a whole wardrobe of colorful size two overalls may not want to hear from the caregiver about the need for a change of style. Be gentle with parents who seem to be stubborn about such suggestions.

Cognitive Readiness

Physical readiness is not enough—cognitive readiness is also necessary. The child must both be capable of using the toilet or potty and understand that is what he or she is to do. Being in child care facilitates this understanding as children see other children in training and model themselves after older classmates. Such an opportunity is an added advantage of multiage settings.

Emotional Readiness

Most important of all is emotional readiness. If a child understands and is capable but is not *willing*, the child is not completely ready. Delays in emotional readiness sometimes occur because toilet training started too soon and the child was pushed too hard. The child may feel a power struggle over using the toilet. If that is the case, the best approach is to lay off for a while and continue to strive for a partnership in the toileting process. Eventually most children will stop being negative about using the toilet. Of course, the power struggle is more likely to be between the child and parent, and the caregiver may not have much control over what is happening there. Conferring with the parent(s) may help.

Parental Viewpoints

It is important that the caregiver discusses toilet training with the parent(s) before any difficult situations arise. The caregiver needs to explain his or her philosophy and find out the parents' ideas, perceptions, and goals for their child in this area of development. When viewpoints differ, the caregiver should try to see the issue from the parents' perspective.

Often a problem occurs when the parents and the caregiver have different definitions of toilet training. The following definition is the

The needed control for using the toilet comes later to some children than to others.

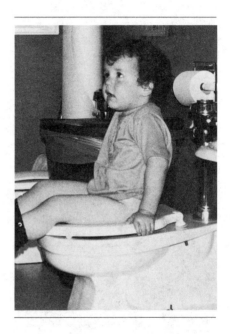

The child may feel a power struggle over using the toilet.

one accepted by most caregivers: Toilet training is the process by which a child learns to take responsibility for his or her own elimination. Toilet training is complete when the child can get to the toilet independently, take off his or her own clothes enough to use the toilet properly, and wipe, flush, and wash his or her hands afterwards.

Some parents see toilet training very differently. They see it as something for which the adult has primary responsibility. Readiness is not a concern. The goal is dry clothes rather than the child's independence. Parents with this view sometimes start toilet training at the end of the first year of life or earlier. Some parents are successful in "catching" their child and putting him or her on the toilet and therefore are able to minimize or eliminate the need for diapers. This method is common practice in many parts of the world and is not that unusual in this country.

Most parents who define toilet training in such a way probably do not ask caregivers to take the responsibility for "catching" their child because of the number of children in the program. Parents may, however, think caregivers know less than they do about infant care; parents may even regard caregivers as lazy because they start toilet training so "late." It is important to work through conflicts such as these and reach some sort of understanding that satisfies both the parent and the caregiver and also takes the child's and the program's needs into consideration.

Emotional Issues

Feelings are an important consideration in any discussion of toilet training. Bodily functions in general, and toileting specifically, call forth many adult feelings. Many adults had harsh toilet training experiences as children and react today out of those experiences even though the reaction is inappropriate for the immediate situation. Many adults were taught that bodily functions are "dirty" and "shameful." Anyone who is going into infant or toddler care needs to become aware of his or her attitude toward such fundamental issues and come to grips with and resolve the leftover feelings that can be passed on to children.

It is vital to children's emotional development that children accept their bodies, the functions of those bodies, and the products of those functions as wholesome, healthy parts of themselves. Children can do that only if the adults around them are positive or at least matter-of-fact about changing and training them. The words adults use reflect their attitudes. Avoid words like *stinky, filthy, disgusting,* and *gross* at the diapering counter or in the bathroom. (Children must, however, be taught sanitary procedures, but this can be done without words that have negative connotations. There is more on this subject in the chapter "Preparing, Ordering, and Maintaining the Environment.")

Parents and caregivers may have different definitions of toilet training.

38

Make toilet learning a pleasant experience. Do not push the child. Be matter-of-fact about accidents. Do not scold or punish. The less emotion involved, the more likely you will stay out of a power struggle that you cannot win. After all, eliminating is one process you cannot control in another person, and it is one in which children can take the upper hand if they feel a need to.

To help toddlers with toilet learning, low child seats are far preferable to child-sized seats on adult-sized toilets. Children have to be lifted on and off the higher seats and may feel very insecure while up there. That insecurity may inhibit their muscle control and work against the toilet training.

Make toilet learning a pleasant experience.

Pay attention to the child's accomplishments but do not get overly emotional about them. For example, briefly praise beginners for telling you after they have filled their diapers. Mention how pleased you are when a child has been dry for several hours. And, of course, you make a big fuss (but not too big) when the child eliminates in the potty or toilet for the first time.

Let the child's readiness be your guide when to begin toilet training. However, consult with the parents about the child's readiness. That ensures their cooperation, and the child feels a consistency between home and the child care program, which makes for more effective learning.

Recording the Information

As is true with feeding, the more communication between parent(s) and caregiver about diapering and toileting, the better. Information should be exchanged about the consistency and frequency of stools and, for the very young breast-fed baby, the frequency of urination (how wet the diapers are indicates how much breast milk the baby is getting). The more both the caregiver and parent know what to expect, the more easily they can meet the individual child's needs.

A simple chart by the diapering counter or bathroom will do to record information concerning the time of changes, the time of bowel movement(s), and anything unusual about the stool. For the toddler in training, the chart can be simpler, merely noting the number of times the child went to the bathroom and when the child moved his or her bowels.

The more communication between parent(s) and caregiver about diapering and toileting, the better.

The information should be available to the parent at pickup time. It may be included with the feeding record or be posted at the diapering area, with a note for the parents near the sign-out sheet if something unusual needs to be brought to their attention. For children in training, it is important to know the last time they went to the bathroom and whether they need some reminding or direction.

When children are cared for by more than one adult, records become important daily sources of information. Without them a child might become constipated because the center thought the child was moving his or her bowels at home and the parent(s) thought the child was doing it at the center. Or a child who is just learning to use the toilet might have an accident on the way home because no one realized that several hours had elapsed since the child had gone to the toilet.

Points to Consider

1. Are you aware of the emotional climate around diapering and toilet training? A positive atmosphere is very important.
2. Do you use diapering times as opportunities for one-to-one interactions when both adult and child are fully attentive to the experience?
3. How well does your diapering and toilet-training routine fit into the overall program structure and philosophy?
4. Does each child enjoy the consistency in diapering and toilet-training approaches that comes from good communication between parent(s) and caregiver?
5. What ideas do you have for resolving the conflicts that may arise when parent(s) and caregiver disagree on the timing or procedures of diapering or toilet training?

Suggested Resources

Books and Articles

Cole, Joanna. *Parents' Book of Toilet Training*. New York: Ballantine Books, Inc., 1988.

Emphasizes waiting until a child is physically, cognitively, and emotionally ready for toilet training.

Gerber, Magda. "Caring for Infants with Respect: The RIE Approach," *Zero to Three* (February, 1984), 1–3.

Presents Magda Gerber's approach to caring for infants and toddlers: she recommends that caregivers always respect babies.

Gonzalez-Mena, Janet, and Dianne W. Eyer. *Infants, Toddlers, and Caregivers*. Mountain View, Calif.: Mayfield Publishing Co., 1989.

Discusses diapering infants and toddlers and toilet training as part of the caregiving routines that make up a major part of the child care curriculum.

Infant and Toddler Program Quality Review Instrument. Sacramento: California State Department of Education, 1988.

Provides guidelines for assessing the quality of programs for infants and toddlers.

Leach, Penelope. *Your Baby and Child: From Birth to Age Five*. New York: Alfred A. Knopf, Inc., 1978.

Offers practical, useful advice about the care of babies.

Leavitt, Robin L., and Brenda K. Eheart. "Managing Routines Within the Daily Schedule," in *Toddler Day Care: A Guide to Responsive Caregiving*. Lexington, Mass.: Lexington Books, 1985, pp. 52–54.

Covers basic sanitation procedures as well as steps to take to diaper a child in a respectful way.

A Manual for Parents and Professionals. Edited by Magda Gerber. Los Angeles: Resources for Infant Educarers, 1978.

Explains how the RIE method works and gives practical advice about how to put respect into caregiving routines such as diapering. Available from Resources for Infant Educarers (RIE), 1550 Murray Circle, Los Angeles, CA 90026.

Samuels, Mike, and Nancy Samuels. *The Well Baby Book*. New York: Summit Books, 1979.

Examines babies' needs and health issues from a holistic health perspective.

Thoman, Evelyn B., and Sue Browder. *Born Dancing: The Relaxed Parents' Guide to Making Babies Smart with Love*. New York: Harper and Row Pubs., Inc., 1987.

Explores how babies communicate and describes how caregivers can trust, respect, and understand babies' unspoken language and natural rhythms, thus engaging in a dance with the infants.

Visions for Infant/Toddler Care: Guidelines for Professional Caregiving. Sacramento: California State Department of Education, 1988.

Presents goals or visions for quality care of infants and toddlers, which should be considered by caregivers and directors of child care.

Audiovisuals

Day to Day with Your Child (Program 2): *The Infant's Communication*. Mount Kisco, N.Y.: Guidance Associates, 1977. Filmstrip, color, 34 minutes total (five programs); printed guide.

Deals with the importance of learning and responding to a baby's signals so the baby can develop trust and become self-reliant. Available from Guidance Associates, Communications Park, Box 3000, Mount Kisco, NY 10549. Telephone: (914) 666-4100; (800) 431-1242.

Flexible, Fearful, or Feisty: The Different Temperaments of Infants and Toddlers. Sacramento: California State Department of Education, 1990. Videocassette, color, 29 minutes; printed guide.

Identifies nine temperamental traits exhibited by infants and toddlers that are typically grouped into three temperamental types, described in the video as flexible, fearful, and feisty. Provides caregivers with techniques for dealing with the differences between individual infants and toddlers in group child care settings.

Getting in Tune: Creating Nurturing Relationships with Infants and Toddlers. Child Care Video Magazine. Sacramento: California State Department of Education, 1988. Videocassette, color, 24 minutes; printed guide.

Presents the "responsive process," which includes three steps: watching, asking, and adapting. Helps the caregiver learn what a young child needs and how best to respond to that need.

Infant Care (Program 1): *Daily Care of the Infant.* Tuckahoe, N.Y.: Campus Films Distributors Corp., 1977. Filmstrip, color, 10 minutes; sound on cassette; printed guide.

Shows the importance of loving interactions during routines of bathing, diapering, and dressing. Includes safety considerations. Available from Campus Films Distributors Corp., 24 Depot Sq., Tuckahoe, NY 10107.

It's Not Just Routine: Feeding, Diapering, and Napping Infants and Toddlers. Sacramento: California State Department of Education, 1990. Videocassette, color, 24 minutes; printed guide.

Demonstrates how to carry out diapering routines with infants and toddlers. Particular attention is given to the setting, safety and health issues, and the quality of the experience for the child and the caregiver.

Respectfully Yours: Magda Gerber's Approach to Professional Infant/Toddler Care. Child Care Video Magazine. Sacramento: California State Department of Education, 1988. Videocassette, color, 55 minutes; printed guide.

Presents Magda Gerber's philosophy based on respecting the baby.

Space to Grow: Creating a Child Care Environment for Infants and Toddlers. Sacramento: California State Department of Education, 1988. Videocassette, color, 22 minutes; printed guide.

Presents eight environmental issues that need to be considered when arranging an environment for infants and toddlers.

The Toddler (Program 1): *Responsibility and Self-reliance*. Tuckahoe, N.Y.: Campus Films Distributors Corp., 1977. Filmstrip, color, 10 minutes; sound on cassette; printed guide.

Describes the pleasure toddlers derive from their developing abilities to brush teeth, dress, help to clean up, and use the toilet. Encourages patience in adults dealing with toddlers. (*Note*: Toilet learning may begin more appropriately a few months later than shown in this filmstrip.) Available from Campus Films Distributors Corp., 24 Depot Sq., Tuckahoe, NY 10707.

Section Four: Dressing and Bathing

essing and bathing are examples of those one-to-one experiences that are so vital to good child care. These routines can be a source of pleasure for the caregiver and the child if the child is encouraged to become involved in the process. Dressing and bathing are also good opportunities for the child to learn body parts because the body can be discussed naturally during both routines.

Dressing and Undressing

Dressing and undressing allow time not only to change the child's clothes but to respond to the child as well. With the young infant, pay attention to babbles and coos and enjoy and return smiles. If the mobile infant starts a peek-a-boo game, pick up on it. With toddlers, be responsive to games they may initiate; for instance, which arm or leg to dress first or which piece of clothing to put on first. These types of responses come naturally to most adults but are mentioned here because when you are responsible for several children and the day gets hectic, you may rush through tasks such as dressing instead of relaxing and doing what comes naturally and takes extra time.

Dressing and bathing are examples of those one-to-one experiences that are so vital to good child care.

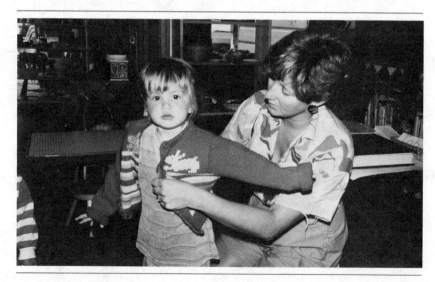

44

Young Infants

Dressing young infants is a little like dressing dolls. Their thumbs stick out at odd angles and catch in sleeves. Their elbows and knees do not bend precisely when you need them to. You need to handle infants and talk to them as human beings, not as lifeless objects. The respect you give early on pays off later as infants gain control of their thumbs and knees. They become cooperative partners before you realize they have, and the hand you struggled so hard with last month slides easily into the sleeve on its own accord this month.

Many young infants dislike being bare and may cry during the changing process. Even though they may be unhappy and you are anxious to get the task over with, it is still important to be respectful. Tell them what you are going to do before you do it: "I'm going to pull your arm through the sleeve now." Try for cooperation: "I've taken your sock halfway off—can you pull it the rest of the way?" Accept their feelings: "I know you don't like this, but we'll be finished in a minute." Talking to babies too young to understand may seem strange, but the understanding comes sooner than you realize— and it comes because you have been talking to the babies from the beginning.

You may also feel guilty doing something you enjoy—such as playing with a single baby—when you "should be working." Remember, you *are* working when you are playing with babies one at a time. You are doing very important work.

Mobile Infants

Young infants just lie there until they learn to cooperate, but mobile infants (who are capable of cooperating) often try to get away. The trick is to contain them long enough to pull off a wet shirt or to put on a sweater to go outside. But the same principles still hold. Treat the infants with respect, try for cooperation, and accept their feelings.

You are likely to get more cooperation in undressing than in dressing; pulling off a hat or shoe is easier than putting one on. Realize that pulling off clothes is the first step, and even when it occurs at unplanned and unnecessary times, the infant is developing important skills. Babies do not pull clothes off to annoy you, they do it because they are practicing—unless you have made such a fuss in the past that they do it to get your attention. If that happens, be sure to stop making a fuss following undressing and start giving plenty of close attention to the child at other times. While you are living through the undressing period of some children, try to remember that dressing skills will eventually follow.

Mobile infants who are willing can easily push arms through armholes and legs into pants. They are probably interested in working on

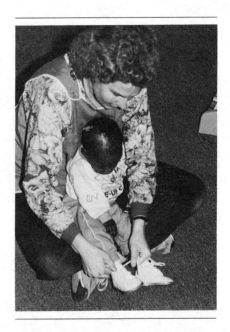

Pulling off a hat or shoe is easier than putting one on.

zippers that you have started if there is a big enough tab to grasp. They can untie shoes, but tying comes much later, as does buttoning and snapping. You can help the process by having available for practice dolls with easy-to-handle clothes and button boards or frames with a variety of fasteners, such as buttons, snaps, and hooks.

Toddlers

Toddlers have increased dressing skills, and some children may be able to dress themselves if the clothes are simple and large enough. Most toddlers, however, still need help. How much or little toddlers cooperate depends on how willing they are. If they are in the stage of finding out the extent of their power to say no, they may well go in the opposite direction when you mention the need to change a shirt or put on a sweater.

Even when toddlers are uncooperative, you must treat them with respect. After you catch them, you can explain that you see how negative they feel about changing but that the change is important for whatever reason: "I see you really don't want to put on your sweater, but it is too cold to go outside without it. I won't let you go outside without your sweater on." If you can give toddlers an acceptable alternative, do so. Having a choice helps children feel more powerful: "You can stay in if you don't want to put your sweater on." "You have to change your shirt, but you can choose the red one or the blue one to change into."

A child's whole day may be ruined by having to wear a shirt that does not belong to him or her. (That is a good reason to have parents bring extra clothes.) Or a toddler new to the program may mightily resist taking a sweater off. The child may feel the stay is temporary if only he or she can manage to leave the sweater on. Perhaps the sweater gives the child comfort, like a security blanket. If that is the case, it is probably worth letting the child leave the sweater on even if the child gets hot.

Some children dislike wearing short sleeves or short pants. Perhaps the air on their arms or legs makes them feel vulnerable. *Other children find certain materials uncomfortable against their skin. Skin sensitivity varies.* Imagine how you would suffer if a wool sweater made you itch and you could not take it off. Try to understand a child's strong opinion about clothes. You may not be able to go along with every whim, but if you make an effort to see things from the individual's point of view, you might find ways to be flexible about issues that really matter to the child. A child's personal preferences are often related to his or her temperament. For more information about temperaments, refer to the video *Flexible, Fearful, or Feisty, The Different Temperaments of Infants and Toddlers* and the book *Infant/Toddler Caregiving: A Guide to Social-Emotional Growth and Socialization.*

Children become used to and usually accept routines.

46

Dressing is a good time for the child to learn body parts because they can be talked about naturally during this routine. Dressing also gives the child opportunities for sensory experience.

Although you always stress self-help skills, sometimes you have to weigh the need for competence against the need for nurturance. If a toddler says, "I can't; you do it," when sitting by the door with shoes in his or her hands, ordinarily you might say, "You put them on, and I'll tie them." But if the child is having a hard day or is ordinarily competent and self-sufficient, you might say, for a change, "I know you can do it, but I see you need me to do it for you this time."

In any routine, making a smooth transition from other activities helps. It is very difficult for a child suddenly to be pulled indoors from a happy time at the water table to have his or her clothes changed. A warning and a waiting period helps: "I am going to have to change your clothes in a few minutes." Sometimes you can catch the child between activities: "I see you're finished at the water table. Now I'm going to change your clothes before you ride the tricycle."

When children are used to the idea that one event precedes or follows another, they get used to the routine (and most accept it). For example, children get used to taking off their shoes for naptime, which occurs after lunch. And they know that they put their coats on before going outside.

Your goals and philosophy more than likely reflect independence as a value. That is why you teach the self-help skills involved with dressing. However, it is important for you to realize that not all individuals or cultures value independence equally. Some parents teach *dependence* rather than independence. Those parents may not expect their children to dress themselves even though they are capable of it. The parents may not put any energy into teaching the children and, instead, may do everything for them. You need to recognize the

Sometimes you have to weigh the need for competence against the need for nurturance.

different viewpoints of those parents and respect them. Most parents will not complain if you teach their children self-help skills. Try not to complain if the parents do not encourage the children to use those skills at home.

Bathing

Bathing may be the most pleasurable of the caregiving routines. For that reason it should probably be left to the parent(s) unless you have a special reason to give regular baths in your program. More likely you will give an occasional bath when a child needs it for a special reason. Be aware, however, that even the occasional bath may tread on the parent's territory unless he or she is as convinced as you are that the child needed it.

Differing views on bathing can cause conflicts.

Some cultures do not regard bathing as a daily necessity and feel North Americans overdo the practice. These differing views can cause conflicts. The baby seen by a parent as clean enough may not meet your standards. If you bathe the baby, the parent may take the action as a personal insult—a message that he or she is not taking good enough care of the child. Strong feelings can result from such a situation.

Or the parent may be on the other side of the conflict. Programs often provide sensory experiences that end up being quite messy—finger paint or sand and water play, for example. Parents may be quite distressed when they pick up their child and find him or her in less than the pristine condition in which they delivered the child that morning.

It does not take long to discover which parents have cleanliness expectations. Respond to those expectations by cleaning the child as much as possible or by giving a bath if you have the facilities. Sand in cornrowed hair or stains on clothing may complicate the situation, however. If either of these is a concern of the parents, take steps to prevent such occurrences. Cover the child's clothes or remove them during messy activities. Stay by the child in the sandbox and protect the child. (Toddlers need to be taught from the beginning not to throw sand—it gets in eyes as well as hair.)

Young Infants

The following steps are for bathing very young infants:

1. Make sure the room is warm enough.

2. Have all the supplies you will need at hand. These include tub, pad, mild soap, towel, clean diaper, and clothes. (Never leave a baby alone on a counter or in a tub while you get something you need.)

3. Half fill the baby bathtub with body-temperature water. (A plastic tub on a counter works well, or you can use a sink.) Test

the water with your elbow or wrist. The water should feel warm but not hot.

4. Start with the infant's head. Wash the face with a soft cloth; do not use soap. Some people use sterile cotton instead of the washcloth for washing around the eyes. Clean the ears by using a corner of the washcloth and a finger. Do not stick cotton swabs in the infant's ears. If the hair is to be washed, wash it next by tucking the infant under your arm, supporting the head with one hand. Hold the head over the tub or under the faucet to wet the hair; soap up, rinse, and towel dry.

   Do not worry about touching the soft spot (fontanelle) on the top of the baby's head. A tough membrane protects the brain, so you do not have to be extra careful. You can wash the area as you do the rest of the head.

5. There are two ways to give the rest of the bath. One is to do the washing on the pad outside the tub and to rinse the baby in the tub. The other is to put the infant in the tub, carefully supporting the head with one hand while you wash and rinse with the other. You can use a cloth or just your hand. Be sure to wash and rinse all wrinkles and crevices.

6. Take the baby out of the tub, wrap him or her in a towel, and pat dry. You can apply baby oil or cornstarch if you want to, although neither is really necessary. (Applying something to the infant's skin is a tradition rather than a biological necessity. During the application you can massage the infant for a while, which some adults and some babies enjoy.)

The steps are simple, but bathing a very young baby may not be. Some young babies scream when undressed, which can make bathtime difficult. The temptation is to bathe the baby as fast as possible to get the task over with. There is nothing wrong with speed as long as you are still respectful in the way you treat the baby. As you do in diapering, dressing, and feeding, tell the baby what is going to happen every step of the way. Talk to the baby in soothing tones. Be gentle. Be responsive. The calmer and more relaxed you are, the better. Your calmness helps the infant settle down.

Mobile Infants and Toddlers

Bathing mobile infants and toddlers is easier in some ways than bathing very young infants; in other ways it is harder. Older babies and toddlers are not as delicate and slippery as younger ones, but they may be active and hard to control. They usually love water, but they may be highly resistant to the washing part of a bath—especially to getting their faces washed. The more you can get children to wash themselves, the less resistance you will encounter.

Some children, especially between the ages of one and two years, are fearful of bathing and hair washing.

Some children, especially between the ages of one and two years, are fearful of bathing or hair washing or both. If fear is a problem, try changing the scene. Bathe in a plastic tub if you have been using a regular bathtub or a sink. (Sometimes the water running down the drain scares children—they think they might slip down, too.) Use less water. Try sponge baths for a while. Water play in which the child has freedom to explore and experience the water on his or her own, at times other than bathtime, may help make bathing easier and less frightening.

The bathtub provides older infants and toddlers not only pleasure but also learning experiences. Bathing is the ultimate water play. Children get a science lesson as they discover the properties of water. A few containers and maybe a sponge or two added to the bathwater allow children to pour, dip, sink, float, and squeeze while they are bathing. Of course, you do not want to turn this time entirely into a play session—but it does not hurt if bathing is fun. Keeping in mind that bathing is a goal-oriented activity will keep you on the task.

When bathing older infants and toddlers, safety is a primary concern. The following procedures are some ways to make bathtime safe and healthy:

1. Never leave a child alone in the tub—not even for a moment. As you do with young infants, have at hand everything you will need for the bath.

2. Always test the water to be sure it is the right temperature. Bad burns have resulted from adult carelessness in this regard.

3. Make sure the bottom of the tub is not slippery. Use a rubber mat or nonskid stickers on the bottom.

4. Control the child's behavior in the tub if he or she tries to stand or gets wild.

5. Use a clean washcloth and towel for each child.

6. Wash the tub thoroughly after each use.

7. Use fresh water for each child.

Bathtime can be a most enjoyable experience for both adult and child. It is another opportunity, as is dressing, for those one-to-one interactions that are so valuable to the child's development.

Points to Consider

1. What can be dangerous about washing and bathing? What precautions can you take to ensure the health and safety of each child you wash, bathe, or dress?

2. How can you make bathing or dressing a respectful experience if the child is crying, resisting, or exhibiting fear?

3. Are you aware of parents' feelings about having their children bathed away from home? Do you have some ideas for solving problems with those parents whose views may be in conflict with yours?

4. How can you make dressing, washing, and bathing more convenient for you and still take a respectful approach to each child?

Suggested Resources

Books and Articles

Gerber, Magda. "Caring for Infants with Respect: The RIE Approach," *Zero to Three* (February, 1984), 1–3.

Presents Magda Gerber's approach to caring for infants and toddlers: she recommends that caregivers always respect babies.

Gonzalez-Mena, Janet, and Dianne W. Eyer. *Infants, Toddlers, and Caregivers.* Mountain View, Calif.: Mayfield Publishing Co., 1989.

Discusses caregiving routines, including dressing, that make up a major part of the child care curriculum.

Infant and Toddler Program Quality Review Instrument. Sacramento: California State Department of Education, 1988.

Provides guidelines for assessing the quality of programs for infants and toddlers.

Infant/Toddler Caregiving: A Guide to Social–Emotional Growth and Socialization. Sacramento: California State Department of Education, 1990.

Presents information on temperaments and offers suggestions for caregiving.

Leach, Penelope. *Your Baby and Child: From Birth to Age Five.* New York: Alfred A. Knopf, Inc., 1978.

Offers practical, useful advice about the care of babies.

A Manual for Parents and Professionals. Edited by Magda Gerber. Los Angeles: Resources for Infant Educarers, 1978.

Explains how the RIE method works and gives practical advice about how to put respect into caregiving routines, such as dressing. Available from Resources for Infant Educarers (RIE), 1550 Murray Circle, Los Angeles, CA 90026.

Samuels, Mike, and Nancy Samuels. *The Well Baby Book.* New York: Summit Books, 1979.

Examines babies' needs and health issues from a holistic health perspective.

Thoman, Evelyn B., and Sue Browder. *Born Dancing: The Relaxed Parents' Guide to Making Babies Smart with Love.* New York: Harper and Row Pubs., Inc., 1987.

Explores how babies communicate and describes how caregivers can trust, respect, and understand babies' unspoken language and natural rhythms, thus engaging in a dance with the infants.

Visions for Infant/Toddler Care: Guidelines for Professional Caregiving. Sacramento: California State Department of Education, 1988.

Presents goals or visions for quality care of infants and toddlers, which should be considered by caregivers and directors of child care.

Audiovisuals

Day Care: A Comprehensive Look—Infants and Toddlers (Part I). Tuckahoe, N.Y.: Campus Films Distributors Corp., 1979. Filmstrip, color, 90 slides; sound on cassette; printed guide.

Discusses the importance of attending to the total development of the child. Emphasizes the importance of daily routines as a time for children to learn and acquire good feelings about the world. Available from Campus Films Distributors Corp., 24 Depot Sq., Tuckahoe, NY 10707.

Day to Day with Your Child (Program 2): *The Infant's Communication.* Mount Kisco, N.Y.: Guidance Associates, 1977. Filmstrip, color, 34 minutes total (five programs); printed guide.

Deals with the importance of learning and responding to a baby's signals so the baby can develop trust and become self-reliant. Available from Guidance Associates, Communications Park, Box 3000, Mount Kisco, NY 10549. Telephone: (914) 666-4100; (800) 431-1242.

Flexible, Fearful, or Feisty: The Different Temperaments of Infants and Toddlers. Sacramento: California State Department of Education, 1990. Videocassette, color, 29 minutes; printed guide.

Identifies nine temperamental traits exhibited by infants and toddlers that are typically grouped into three temperamental types, described in the video as flexible, fearful, and feisty. Provides caregivers with techniques for dealing with the differences between individual infants and toddlers in group child care settings.

Getting in Tune: Creating Nurturing Relationships with Infants and Toddlers. Child Care Video Magazine. Sacramento: California State Department of Education, 1988. Videocassette, color, 24 minutes; printed guide.

Presents the "responsive process," which includes three steps: watching, asking, and adapting. Helps the caregiver learn what a young child needs and how best to respond to that need.

Infant Care (Program 1): *Daily Care of the Infant.* Tuckahoe, N.Y.: Campus Films Distributors Corp., 1977. Filmstrip, color, 10 minutes; sound on cassette; printed guide.

Shows the importance of loving interactions during routines of bathing, diapering, and dressing. Includes safety considerations. Available from Campus Films Distributors Corp., 24 Depot Sq., Tuckahoe, NY 10707.

Respectfully Yours: Magda Gerber's Approach to Professional Infant/Toddler Care. Child Care Video Magazine. Sacramento: California State Department of Education, 1988. Videocassette, color, 55 minutes; printed guide.

Presents Magda Gerber's philosophy based on respecting the baby.

The Toddler (Program 1): *Responsibility and Self-reliance.* Tuckahoe, N.Y.: Campus Films Distributors Corp., 1977. Filmstrip, color, 10 minutes; sound on cassette; printed guide.

Describes the pleasure toddlers derive from their developing abilities to brush teeth, dress, help to clean up, and use the toilet. Encourages patience in adults dealing with toddlers. Available from Campus Films Distributors Corp., 24 Depot Sq., Tuckahoe, NY 10707.

Section Five: Sleeping and Naptime

Rest needs vary greatly from the two-month-old to the three-year-old and from one individual to another, regardless of age. Most infants need a good deal more sleep than toddlers. It is vital that infants be allowed to establish and maintain their own sleeping schedules and not be expected to conform to a group schedule. For older toddlers you can establish a regular afternoon naptime routine rather than continue the individual schedules for each child. However, the environment should be set up to allow both mobile infants and toddlers to seek out soft, quiet, out-of-the-way spaces to rest whenever the need arises.

Young Infants

The primary requirements for meeting young infants' sleeping needs are a sensitive caregiver who can read each child's signals and a safe, comfortable, familiar place to sleep.

Infants should not be in cribs unless they are ready to go to sleep. If you make a distinction between the place to play and the place to sleep, infants will go to sleep more easily. Nonmobile infants need to spend waking hours lying in safe places where they can look around, use their hands, kick their feet, and change positions freely. They should also be in close contact with their caregivers and other children. Appropriate places for awake, nonmobile infants are on the floor, in playpens, outside on a blanket on the grass, or in an open carriage under a tree—but not in a crib. An adult must take responsibility for noting when a child needs to sleep and put that child in his or her own crib.

Clues to Sleepiness

You can easily tell when young infants are sleepy if they yawn, rub their eyes, or drift off. But what about a baby who is screaming at the top of his or her lungs or fussing unhappily? How can you tell whether sleep is what the child needs?

One way to know is by what the parents tell you. Many parents are quite tuned in to their baby's individual cues and schedules. The parents know that the reason the baby cries about 10 a.m. is that the

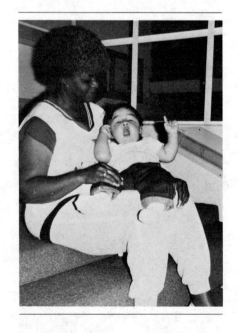

baby is tired. Maybe the baby was up most of the night. If you have that information in the morning, you will know that when the baby cries after drinking the bottle, the child is most likely sleepy. You will know that the most appropriate action is to put the baby in the crib and expect him or her to sleep.

What if the infant does not sleep but continues to cry? What do you do then? What you do depends again on your knowledge of that particular infant. Perhaps you have been told by the parent or know from experience that the baby needs to fuss for a few minutes before settling down to sleep. If that is the case, then the baby needs to stay in the crib and fuss. Or you may know that once a particular child starts crying, the child gets so worked up that he or she takes a long time to settle down to sleep. You will take that child out of the crib and find ways to relax and comfort the child until he or she can again be put down to sleep. Perhaps you know (from the parents or from experience) that this particular baby goes to sleep faster if rocked. In that case you will rock the baby.

During the transition from being awake to falling asleep, trust is important in infants (and toddlers). Trust, which allows children to let go and fall asleep, develops most easily for many children with a primary caregiver system. This system encourages attachment to one special caregiver and supports the development of trust. Thus at sleeping times, when children often feel the most vulnerable, they are able to relax because their primary caregiver knows and is part of their individual presleep ritual.

Get information about the infant's cues and schedules from the parents.

The Right Environment

The first requirement for meeting young infants' sleeping needs is a primary caregiver who can read the children's signals and who knows each child's routine. The second requirement is a safe, com-

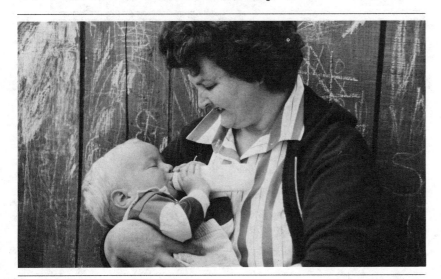

The transition from being awake to falling asleep is a time when trust is important.

fortable, familiar place to sleep. The younger the infant the more likely that a small, confined area, such as a bassinet or a baby carriage, will provide a sense of security. Some young infants fear wide open spaces, and even a crib feels unsafe to them.

Other young infants are stimulated by the views a crib affords of other cribs and other babies and have a hard time sleeping under the circumstances. Crib bumpers can help restrict the infant's view; bumpers need to be used for young infants, anyway, because infants squirm up to the hard bars as they sleep. After a few months, the size of the space becomes less of a problem, but visual stimulation—no longer hidden by bumpers—can remain a problem through the toddler years.

Because cribs are reserved for sleeping, toys, other than ones that are soft and comforting for the child, belong elsewhere, as do exciting, interesting pictures and other visual enticements. Colors in sleeping areas should be toned down—the bright reds, yellows, and oranges sometimes found in infant care environments especially need to be kept out of the sleeping areas. Noise should be minimal, too.

Some cultures view outdoor sleeping as healthier than indoor sleeping. Child care centers in some countries have outdoor sleeping areas for summer and sleeping porches with screens instead of windows for winter. Although such setups are rare or nonexistent in this country, some caregivers who value fresh air do find ways for the youngest infants to sleep outdoors in baby carriages. There is nothing like a slight breeze moving the leaves of a tree to help the baby in a carriage below go to sleep in a few minutes.

Safety considerations are vital when providing for sleeping needs. Never put an infant to bed with a propped bottle; infants have choked because of bottles. Infants need to be held for both safety and psychological reasons when being fed. Be absolutely sure that there are no

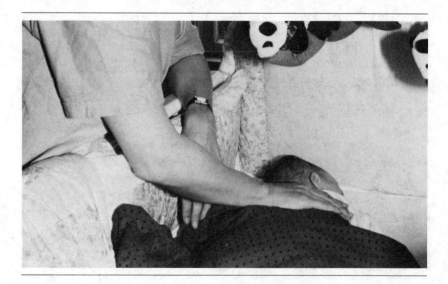

dangling strings in or around the sleeping area. (Cords from curtains or blinds have strangled infants.) Avoid soft cushions or pillows that infants can get wedged under. Use only safety-approved cribs, bassinets, and carriages with properly fitting mattresses. Even then, check the distance between the mattress and sides of the crib and the spacing of the bars. Infants have died from getting their heads caught between crib bars or between the mattress and crib sides.

Be sure that each child sleeps in his or her own bed (crib, bassinet, carriage) each day and that it is in the same place. Familiarity and predictability of the sleep setting are important in forming trust. As infants grow, they become increasingly sensitive to location changes.

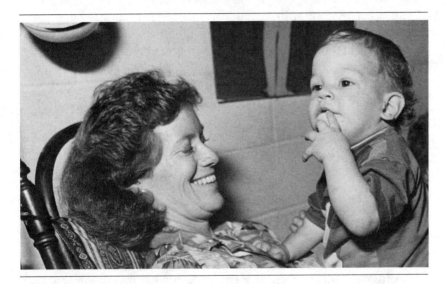

Mobile Infants

The same principles apply to older infants as to younger ones. Mobile infants need sensitive caregivers who can read their signals and understand their individual ways of going to sleep and waking up. Mobile infants also need a safe, quiet, comfortable, familiar place to sleep. The older a child gets, the longer his or her going-to-sleep ritual may become.

The following tips may help mobile infants get to sleep, stay asleep, and wake up in their own individual ways:

1. Do what you can to keep mobile infants from learning how to climb out of their cribs. Get children up right away at the end of naptime instead of leaving them there to figure out how to get out themselves. The exceptions are the children who wake slowly and like to lie and "talk" to themselves, prolonging the transition period.

2. If a child wakes up before fully satisfying his or her sleep needs, you may need to respond by laying the child back down and

telling the child to go back to sleep. Be careful about being too stimulating when you do this. Many children can ease themselves back to sleep if they do not get too wide awake or come to depend too much on you to help them.

3. Find ways to provide visual and auditory privacy for the children who need it. Many children have trouble going to sleep when they can see or hear other children.

Toddlers

By about two years of age, most children are down to one nap a day, in the afternoon, with perhaps some brief rests at other times. Sometime during the second year, the children may move from a crib to a cot or a mat on the floor. Programs that separate toddlers from infants usually do not have nap rooms. Cots are brought out and set up in the playspace. That means naptime must be scheduled for the group instead of allowing individuals to nap according to their own schedules.

Familiarity and predictability of the sleep setting are important in forming trust.

It continues to be important for toddlers to have the same bed in the same place every day. Because toddlers are not usually confined to cribs, getting them to sleep may take some time and energy. You cannot just put toddlers down and know that they will stay there. You need patience, clear, firm messages, and a variety of techniques to get a group of toddlers to sleep.

The following are tips on how to put toddlers down for a nap:

1. Provide a transition period between active play and sleep. Many programs serve lunch right before naptime, providing a change of pace. After lunch and cleanup, children take off their shoes and may be undressed. (Not all programs change clothes for

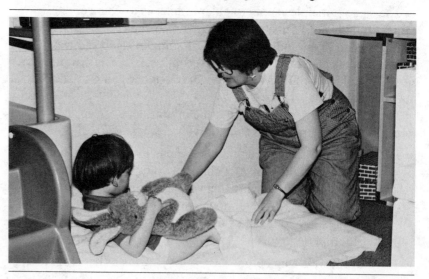

58

sleeping.) These routines provide clues about what is to come and prepare the children to settle down.

2. Change the setting. Put toys away, preferably in closed cabinets. The cots taking over the playspace are a reminder that naptime is approaching. Toward the end of the transition, the lights are usually turned down or the shades are pulled. Some programs play soft music, thus providing a more relaxed atmosphere that gives different messages from the earlier bright, toy-filled setting.

3. Learn which rituals work best with which children. Many children have a favored object or blanket they take to bed with them. Getting the object and snuggling down with it can be part of the ritual. Some children are used to hearing a story before going to sleep. Others are sung to. Some enjoy a back rub, which soothes and relaxes them.

4. Make sure that the toddlers in the program get plenty of fresh air and exercise every day. There is nothing like being tired to provide motivation for going to sleep. However, be careful children do not get overtired. Some toddlers have a very hard time settling down to sleep when overtired.

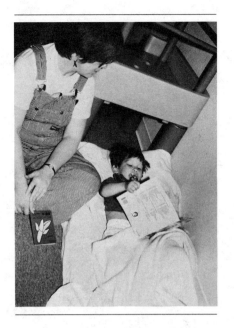

Temperamental Differences

Some infants establish regular schedules and are easy to put down to sleep. Others have irregular schedules, are less predictable, and may resist going to sleep. Both types of children need to be put down to sleep when they are tired, even if they protest.

Some infants are soothed by rocking, rubbing, or being sung to. However, some highly sensitive infants are stimulated rather than soothed by voices, rubbing, or even the presence of other people when trying to go to sleep.

Some infants are more persistent than others in their protests about going to sleep. Do not leave a child to cry for long periods, but do stand firm if sleep is what is needed. Periodically you may gently reassure the child that he or she is not alone, but do not give up on putting the child to sleep.

Waking-up Styles

Some children take long naps; others take shorter ones. You can help to individualize your program by setting up a place for the short nappers to go to so they will not disturb the longer nappers. Some programs send children outside when they wake up (in good weather). Other programs have a room children can go to and play or an area of the room set up for the early risers.

Children wake up in different moods and degrees of readiness for interaction. Some children are slow wakers and need a long transition to lie around and get fully awake. Others bounce up and are ready to resume where they left off playing. Try to be sensitive to these differences.

Resisting Sleep

Some children fight naptime energetically. If the child resisting *needs* the sleep, the situation is different from one in which he or she does not need sleep. You can tell by knowing the child. If the child is particularly fussy or easily frustrated, the chances are the child is fighting sleep for some reason other than that he or she does not need it. Try to find out what the reason is. In the meantime, you need to insist that the child lie down; if he or she refuses, you may have to sit next to the child and keep insisting firmly and calmly. (Getting upset wakes the child even more.)

You may get some clues about the situation from the child's parent(s). Explain the problem to them and ask their ideas about what is causing the problem and what to do about it. The difficulty may be environmental. The child may need more isolation than you have been providing. A screen may help. If the problem is insecurity or lack of trust, the solution may take a little longer until the child forms attachments at the center. A transitional object, such as a special toy, blanket, or even a possession of the mother's (for example, a scarf), may help.

The difficulty may be neither environmental nor emotional. Perhaps the child has learned that by staying awake and making a fuss, he or she gets special attention. If the need for attention is the source of the resisting behavior, it is important to remove the attention when the behavior occurs and give the child plenty of extra attention at other times.

Try to be sensitive to different styles of waking up.

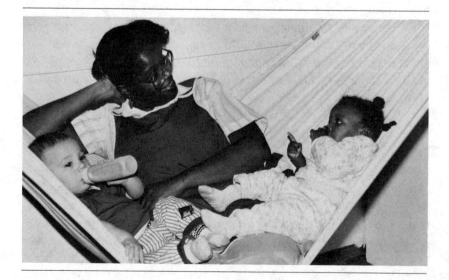

A few children between the ages of two and three years are ready to give up naptime. What you do about this depends on the program and staff needs. Some programs can accommodate differences in napping behavior and see the nonnapping child in a positive light. The program may provide interesting, quiet activities and take advantage of the low child–adult ratio to give the child special attention.

Other programs depend on naptime to meet staff or program needs. If meetings or preparation activities are planned, a wandering child or two can create quite a problem. Also, a wandering child or two may become a whole crowd as the children perceive adults rewarding children who refuse to nap. In some programs staff depend on the quiet time for their own renewal. If that is the case, the policy is to insist all children lie down for a certain amount of time. Most toddlers will fall asleep if you have them spend some time on their cots. Even though they can get along fine without the sleep, toddlers can be encouraged to sleep during the day.

Most toddlers will sleep if they lie down.

The situation is more complicated when the parents' ideas about naptime conflict with those of the staff. Some parents feel it is important not to enforce rest. They believe that it is preferable for children to learn to read their own body signs and rest when they are tired rather than according to the schedule. Other parents have difficulties getting their children to bed at night when the children have a long nap in the afternoon. The parents may request either that you not put the child down at all or that you wake the child up after a certain amount of time.

The parents' scheduling needs may be in direct conflict with the staff schedule and sometimes in conflict with the child's schedule. There are no easy solutions to such a problem. The answer, as always, is to discuss and negotiate. Try to see the parents' point of view and explain yours. Then work together toward a mutually acceptable solution.

Parents and caregivers may have to work together toward a mutually acceptable solution to resolving conflicts over naptime schedules.

Recording the Information

How long their child slept and the time of the most recent awakening can be important information for parents who need to plan the evening with their children. Is the baby likely to be ready for bed soon after dinner or has the child been asleep all afternoon? Did the toddler wake up early from the nap and that is why he or she is sleepy in the car going home? Napping information can be recorded easily in the same manner as feeding and diapering information. When there is consistency of caregivers and good communication, oral reporting is all that is necessary. If you are the primary caregiver and have a good memory, and you are the one who delivers the baby into the arms of the parent, you can simply tell the parent how well the baby napped that day. But using memory alone means you do not have records over a period of time to note patterns and changes in those patterns, which can sometimes be helpful information.

Points to Consider

1. How individualized are your napping routines? Do you allow infants to set their own schedules? Does every child have at least one caregiver who knows his or her unique going-to-sleep and waking-up patterns? If the primary caregiver is not present, is there still consistency in the way the child is put to sleep?

2. How much thought have you given to setting up a safe, cozy, comfortable, and peaceful napping environment for each child?

3. Are the napping routines in child care consistent with the sleeping routines at home? What kind of communication do you have with parents about the child's sleeping needs and napping routines? What process do you have for problem solving in parent–caregiver conflicts over napping issues?

4. How well do the napping routines work for the caregivers in the program?

5. Do the napping routines fit into the overall program structure and philosophy?

Suggested Resources

Books and Articles

Gerber, Magda. "Caring for Infants with Respect: The RIE Approach," *Zero to Three* (February, 1984), 1–3.

Presents Magda Gerber's approach to caring for infants and toddlers: she recommends that caregivers always respect babies.

Gonzalez-Mena, Janet, and Dianne W. Eyer. *Infants, Toddlers, and Caregivers.* Mountain View, Calif.: Mayfield Publishing Co., 1989.

Discusses caregiving routines that make up a major part of the child care curriculum.

Infant and Toddler Program Quality Review Instrument. Sacramento: California State Department of Education, 1988.

Provides guidelines for assessing the quality of programs for infants and toddlers.

Leach, Penelope. *Your Baby and Child: From Birth to Age Five.* New York: Alfred A. Knopf, Inc., 1978.

Offers practical, useful advice about the care of babies.

Leavitt, Robin L., and Brenda K. Eheart. "Managing Routines Within the Daily Schedule," in *Toddler Day Care: A Guide to Responsive Caregiving.* Lexington, Mass.: Lexington Books, 1985, pp. 51-52.

Provides ideas on how to help toddlers make the transition to naptime and considers the issue of flexibility and sleeping schedules.

A Manual for Parents and Professionals. Edited by Magda Gerber. Los Angeles: Resources for Infant Educarers, 1978.

Explains how the RIE method works and gives practical advice about how to put respect into caregiving routines, such as napping and sleeping. Available from Resources for Infant Educarers (RIE), 1550 Murray Circle, Los Angeles, CA 90026.

Samuels, Mike, and Nancy Samuels. *The Well Baby Book.* New York: Summit Books, 1979.

Examines babies' needs and health issues from a holistic health perspective.

Thoman, Evelyn B., and Sue Browder. *Born Dancing: The Relaxed Parents' Guide to Making Babies Smart with Love.* New York: Harper and Row Pubs., Inc., 1987.

Explores how babies communicate and describes how caregivers can trust, respect, and understand babies' unspoken language and natural rhythms, thus engaging in a dance with the infants.

Visions for Infant/Toddler Care: Guidelines for Professional Caregiving. Sacramento: California State Department of Education, 1988.

Presents goals or visions for quality care of infants and toddlers, which should be considered by caregivers and directors of child care.

Audiovisuals

Babies in Family Day Care. Ithaca, N.Y.: Cornell University AV Center-C, 1979. Filmstrip, color, 93 slides; sound on cassette; printed guide.

Shows the importance of flexible scheduling, close attention, and affection for babies in child care and how the caregiver can successfully provide all these while he or she cares for several children. Describes caregiving environments for children from three months to five years. Available from Cornell University AV Center-C, 8 Research Park, Ithaca, NY 14850.

Day to Day with Your Child (Program 2): *The Infant's Communication.* Mount Kisco, N.Y.: Guidance Associates, 1977. Filmstrip, color, 34 minutes total (five programs); printed guide.

Deals with the importance of learning and responding to a baby's signals so the baby can develop trust and become self-reliant. Available from Guidance Associates, Communications Park, Box 3000, Mount Kisco, NY 10549. Telephone: (914) 666-4100; (800) 431-1242.

Flexible, Fearful, or Feisty: The Different Temperaments of Infants and Toddlers. Sacramento: California State Department of Education, 1990. Videocassette, color, 29 minutes; printed guide.

Identifies nine temperamental traits exhibited by infants and toddlers that are typically grouped into three temperamental types, described in the video as flexible, fearful, and feisty. Provides caregivers with techniques for dealing with the differences between individual infants and toddlers in group child care settings.

Getting in Tune: Creating Nurturing Relationships with Infants and Toddlers. Child Care Video Magazine. Sacramento: California State Department of Education, 1988. Videocassette, color, 24 minutes; printed guide.

Presents the "responsive process," which includes three steps: watching, asking, and adapting. Helps the caregiver learn what a young child needs and how best to respond to that need.

It's Not Just Routine: Feeding, Diapering, and Napping Infants and Toddlers. Sacramento: California State Department of Education, 1990. Videocassette, color, 24 minutes; printed guide.

Demonstrates how to carry out sleeping and napping routines with infants and toddlers. Particular attention is given to the setting, safety and health issues, and the quality of the experience for the child and the caregiver.

Respectfully Yours: Magda Gerber's Approach to Professional Infant/Toddler Care. Child Care Video Magazine. Sacramento: California State Department of Education, 1988. Videocassette, color, 55 minutes; printed guide.

Presents Magda Gerber's philosophy based on respecting the baby.

Section Six: Preparing, Ordering, and Maintaining the Environment

Planning and keeping an appropriate environment is an ongoing caregiver task. The environment should be set up for various activities during the day, flexible to meet individual needs, and changed on a regular basis, when necessary. In the early morning, you can set up cushions and pillows and cozy corners and expect snuggling and "reading" activities to take precedence over more active play. Later, breakfast routines will change the environment. After breakfast, most programs encourage free play, which usually involves more gross motor activity on the part of the children. Throughout the day, routines dictate the setup of the environment unless, of course, you have a different room for each routine.

Periodically you must check to be sure the environment is safe, sanitary, and developmentally appropriate. (Developmentally appropriate means there are the right kinds of toys and equipment for the age group served.) Most programs have a daily safety and sanitary check. Developmental appropriateness should be checked weekly for young and mobile infants and monthly for toddlers, except when new children enter the program; in that case, you must give immediate attention to the newcomers' developmental needs.

Children, even from a young age, can begin to develop some sense of responsibility for the environment they inhabit.

Children's Involvement

Keeping the environment clean and in good order is an ongoing caregiving routine, one in which you want to keep the children involved. Children pick up attitudes very quickly. If you are convinced that the responsibility is theirs as well as yours, they will be too. But if you approach cleanup with a negative state of mind, children are likely to resist. If you make cleaning up interesting and fun, they do not see it as a chore but as a chance to get involved in helping you.

The age of the child influences how much help he or she will be. Children, even from a young age, can begin to develop some sense of responsibility for the environment they inhabit. Young infants, of course, will only watch the proceedings. But mobile infants are good imitators, and if you start putting toys on the shelves or balls back into a basket, you are likely to get cooperation from some "helpers." Toddlers can be even more useful, matching toys to their pictures on the shelves and sorting bean bags from balls.

Order and Freedom

It is important that the environment is organized but not so organized that the children are discouraged from exploring. There is a delicate balance between maintaining order and giving freedom.

Obviously children cannot explore a puzzle if the pieces are scattered to the distant corners of the room. Beginning walkers cannot navigate a rug so littered with toys that they cannot find a space to put a foot. Yet if you keep order with too heavy a hand, either the children will be too inhibited to explore or they will make a game of destroying the order that you are pushing on them.

The nature of the activities that mobile infants and toddlers engage in makes maintaining order hard. One such activity is dumping. A bucket or basket of objects invites dumping. The child may also refill the container, in which case the activity becomes a cycle—a dump–fill cycle. The problem is that because the activity is a *cycle,* the child is as likely to dump again as to put the container back on the shelf. If the child happens to grow tired of the activity at the end of the fill part of the cycle, you are lucky, but the chances are that the child will wander off after the last dump rather than the last fill, unless your timing is superb and you intervene.

Another activity common to mobile infants and toddlers is pick up–carry–drop. When children begin to move around, they like to take objects with them. For instance, if you watch fourteen-month-olds, you will see that they often have in their hands objects that they drop or place on the floor in order to pick up another object. While charting this behavior, you may discover that a child may pick up, carry around, and put down as many as 20 objects in 15 minutes. That

There is a delicate balance between maintaining order and giving freedom.

66

means if you are trying to keep everything in its place when it is not being played with, you are going to have a hard time.

Pickup Time

Periodically throughout the day the toys get put back into their places on the shelves during what is known as "pickup time." The event to follow is usually exciting enough (such as going outside, going for a walk, having lunch) that the pickup is done in eager anticipation.

Children, especially toddlers, can be involved in more of the cleanup routine than just picking up toys. Toddlers can clear the table after lunch, deposit the dishes in an available container, and even sponge off their places at the table. Getting the children to do this takes some teaching and modeling, but if your directions are clear and simple, most toddlers enjoy not only the responsibility but the sensory aspects that go along with cleanup. (Sponging can be a very satisfying activity.)

Extent of Involvement

How involved the children are in preparing the environment depends on the program. Participation in routines is a major part of the curriculum for infants and toddlers. Some programs have a period before the children arrive to arrange and set things up for the day. Others are set up so that caregivers arrive with the children. In that case arranging equipment and setting out toys and activities may involve the children who arrive early unless the task is done by the last person to leave at night.

If you include children in cleanup, regarding them as partners from

Participation in routines is a major part of the curriculum for infants and toddlers.

the beginning, you may find that the job takes longer to get done. But the extra time at the beginning is an investment that pays off later. Once children have gained skills, they become effective helpers who can save you time and effort.

Setup and Maintenance

The following are tips for setting up and maintaining an orderly environment that invites exploration:

1. Provide low open shelves to store available toys. If you label (with pictures) the places for each toy, children not only can put the toys back in the right place but will engage them cognitively while they are doing so (matching an object to a symbol).

2. Select a number of toys that allow plenty to do but do not put out every toy. It is always a good practice to keep supplementary toys in closed cupboards that children cannot reach. Rotating some toys now and then makes the environment interesting for the children.

3. Do not let disorder get beyond the capabilities of the "picker-uppers." Do regular pickup when needed rather than wait until lunchtime. Even a moderately messy room can be overwhelming to toddlers who want to help pick up. If too much of a mess has accumulated, break the activity down to manageable parts, saying, for example, "Let's put all the connecting blocks back in the can" instead of "Let's pick up the toys now."

4. Clean up one thing before starting another. Sometimes timing is such that you cannot quite manage that, but the day does go smoother if you have cleared away the finger paints before you start the lunch preparations.

5. Keep cheerful and positive. Make a game of picking up. Your attitude is important, as is your presence. You cannot tell toddlers to pick up and then turn your back and expect they will do it. You need to be involved, too. Your involvement is part of what makes the activity interesting to them. See picking up as a joint project rather than as the children's responsibility alone.

The video *Space to Grow: Creating a Child Care Environment for Infants and Toddlers* and *Infant/Toddler Caregiving: A Guide to Setting Up Environments* provide many ideas on how to set up and maintain an orderly, effective environment for young infants, mobile infants, and toddlers.

Sanitation Procedures

The sanitary aspects of cleanup necessarily exclude children's help because of the germs and chemicals involved. Because diseases such as hepatitis and giardia are on the increase, sanitation is essential to everyone's health. The following recommended routines will help prevent the spread of illness:

1. Keep floors clean: vacuum rugs daily; sweep and mop floors daily or after meals, when necessary; clean up spills as they occur.

2. Remove shoes from everyone walking in areas where young infants lie. Soft washable slippers with nonskid soles are recommended for caregivers.

3. Wash toys and equipment daily. Use soap and water if toys are sticky or dirty, followed by a bleach solution. If there are no signs of dirt, use a bleach solution alone. Some programs' staff regularly run plastic toys through the dishwasher.

4. Use the sanitary diapering procedures outlined in "Diapering and Toileting."

5. Carefully wash bottles and eating utensils and sanitize them either with a bleach solution or in a dishwasher with extra hot water.

6. Store opened or prepared food and bottles in the refrigerator at all times. Date items that go in so you can keep track of what is old.

7. Change bed linens regularly.

Safety Procedures

Safety is as important as sanitation. The following are some safety guidelines:

1. Cover all electrical outlets within the children's reach.

2. Remove all dangling cords and strings.

3. Formulate a plan in case of fire. Be sure all exit doors are clear. Organize a system for getting all children out. Equip the room(s) with smoke detectors, fire alarms, fire extinguishers, and fire blankets.

4. All glass in reach of children (windows, mirrors, aquariums, etc.) should be shatterproof or protected.

5. Find out which houseplants are poisonous (many are) and remove them.

6. Check outdoors for poisonous plants and remove them.

7. Keep all equipment in good repair and check regularly.

8. Cover all heaters or protect them in some way.

9. Keep all cleaning supplies, medicines, and the staff's personal belongings away from the children. Those materials need to be locked away so children cannot possibly get to them.

10. Make sure all toys and equipment are age-appropriate for the children in the environment.

Points to Consider

1. Do your cleanup routines reflect the philosophy and goals of your program?

2. Are health and safety considerations part of your cleanup routine?

3. Do you make provisions for all children to participate in cleanup, with each child at the appropriate developmental level of involvement?

4. How do you decide among staff what standards of orderliness are acceptable to all? Do you have a problem-solving process to work on conflicts?

Suggested Resources

Books and Articles

Ferguson, J. "Creating Growth-producing Environments for Infants and Toddlers," in *Supporting the Growth of Infants, Toddlers and Parents.* Edited by E. Jones. Pasadena, Calif.: Pacific Oaks College, 1979, pp. 13–26.

Provides an overview of vital concerns in creating an environment for infants and toddlers.

Gonzalez-Mena, Janet, and Dianne W. Eyer. *Infants, Toddlers, and Caregivers.* Mountain View, Calif.: Mayfield Publishing Co., 1989.

Discusses environments from the point of view of caregiving, free play, health, and safety.

Greenman, J. "Babies Get Out," *Beginnings* (Summer, 1985).

Explores the value of taking infants and toddlers outdoors and offers practical suggestions on how to make available and enhance outdoor experience for young children.

Greenman, J. *Caring Spaces, Learning Places: Children's Environments That Work.* Redmond, Wash.: Exchange Press, Inc., 1988.

Discusses how to design and redesign center places and spaces for children and adults.

Infant/Toddler Caregiving: A Guide to Setting Up Environments. Sacramento: California State Department of Education, 1990.

Presents ideas and suggestions for setting up and maintaining a rich, age-appropriate environment for infants and toddlers. Includes many photographs and illustrations.

Olds, A. R. "Designing Play Environments for Children Under Three," *Topics in Early Childhood Special Education*, Vol. 2 (1982), 87–95.

Discusses what to consider when designing environments for infants and toddlers.

Willis, Anne, and Henry Ricciuti. *A Good Beginning for Babies: Guidelines for Group Care.* Washington, D.C.: National Association for the Education of Young Children, 1975.

Includes guidelines for physical space, equipment, health, and safety.

Audiovisuals

Babies in Family Day Care. Ithaca, N.Y.: Cornell University AV Center-C, 1979. Filmstrip, color, 93 slides; sound on cassette; printed guide.

Shows the importance of flexible scheduling, close attention, and affection for babies in child care and how the caregiver can successfully provide all these while he or she cares for several children. Describes caregiving environments for children from three months to five years. Available from Cornell University AV Center-C, 8 Research Park, Ithaca, NY 14850.

A Recipe for Happy Children. A program in "Spoonful of Lovin'." Bloomington, Ind.: Agency for Instructional Television, 1980. Videocassette, 30 minutes.

Emphasizes a safe learning environment and other topics, such as appropriate activities for young children, how to relate to parents, and a positive approach to discipline. Available from Agency for Instructional Television, Box A, Bloomington, IN 47402.

Space to Grow: Creating a Child Care Environment for Infants and Toddlers. Child Care Video Magazine. Sacramento: California State Department of Education, 1988. Videocassette, color, 22 minutes; printed guide.

Discusses setting up and maintaining a rich, age-appropriate environment for infants and toddlers.

The Toddler (Program 1): *Responsibility and Self-Reliance.* Tuckahoe, N.Y.: Campus Films Distributors Corp., 1977. Filmstrip, color, 10 minutes; sound on cassette; printed guide.

Describes the pleasure toddlers derive from their developing abilities to participate in activities that concern them, including cleaning up. Encourages patience in adults dealing with toddlers. Available from Campus Films Distributors Corp., 24 Depot Sq., Tuckahoe, NY 10707.

Section Seven: Health and Safety

Health and safety issues often overshadow the normal caregiving routines. In some cases, those concerns may alter the way in which a particular routine is handled. Health and safety are serious matters that need to be thoughtfully integrated into daily routines as much as possible.

As a caregiver it is important that *you* have clearly defined, written health and safety policies and guidelines for your program. Review and revise your policies and guidelines on a regular basis, getting input from your parents, other caregivers, and local health and medical authorities. Be sure all parents and staff in your program have current copies of your policy guidelines. Post a copy with your emergency information by the telephone for easy access.

An important reference guide that will help you develop specific policies is the publication *Healthy Young Children: A Manual for*

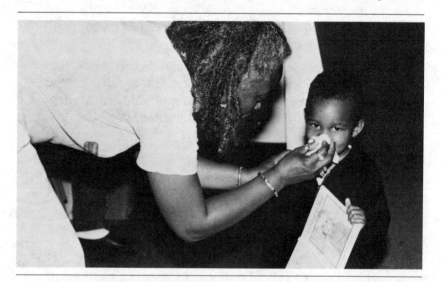

Note: For the health, safety, and well-being of children as well as child care providers, basic health and safety requirements are mandated through legislation, and licensing is usually required for all child care centers and family child care homes. In California, for example, the California State Department of Social Services, Community Care Licensing, is responsible for licensing. In addition, the California State Department of Education's publications *Visions for Infant/Toddler Care: Guidelines for Professional Caregiving* and *Infant and Toddler Program Quality Review Instrument* outline important health and safety program elements. Check in your state for similar mandates, requirements, and guidelines.

Programs, available from the National Association for the Education of Young Children (NAEYC). It is an excellent and comprehensive guide recommended for all programs. The manual details essential policy information and covers a variety of important health and safety issues. The American Academy of Pediatrics is another important source of information on the health, safety, and well-being of children. The academy publishes many pamphlets and flyers that are available free of charge or at minimal cost to caregivers and parents.

Guidelines for a Healthy Environment

The following guidelines, which relate directly to caregiving routines, will assist you in preparing appropriate health policies, procedures, and guidelines for your program.

Sanitation

Sanitation is absolutely necessary for keeping children and caregivers healthy. You can maintain a sanitary environment and prevent cross-contamination by following these recommended procedures:

- Adhere strictly to careful handwashing procedures. This is the single most effective means of preventing the spread of illness. Wash your hands frequently throughout the day as you work with children. In order to prevent cross-contamination, you need to wash your hands:

    1. At the start of the day just before working with the children

    2. Before *and* after handling food and feeding children

    3. Before *and* after diapering/toileting a child

    4. Before *and* after your own toileting and personal grooming

    5. After having contact with any bodily fluids (mucous, saliva, urine)

    Model for the children appropriate handwashing by showing and telling them when *you* are washing your hands after toileting and before eating. Also, with very young children, it is important to show them how to wash their hands by actually washing their hands and explaining what you are doing. Be sure they wash every time after toileting and before eating.

- Maintain a separate area and sink for food preparation and cleanup. The area for toileting and diapering should be equipped with its own sink and be situated away from the food preparation area. A separate area and sink should also be available for facility cleanup. Different cleanup cloths should be used in each of the areas.

- Each day, systematically clean and wash all toys using a dishwasher, clothes washer, and/or bleach solution to sterilize items. Use a solution of 1/4 cup liquid chlorine bleach to one gallon of

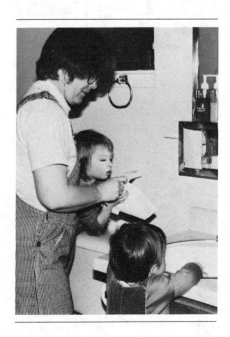

water. The solution must be prepared daily because it weakens over a day's time and will not be strong enough to kill germs. Put the solution in a clearly marked spray bottle for easy use.

• Clean and disinfect all surfaces, including bathrooms, tables, and floors daily.

Diapering and Toileting

• Use only diapering tables or specific areas for diapering and changing children's soiled clothing. Clean the tables with bleach solution after *each use*. Dispose of soiled diapers in a diaper pail or garbage can that is convenient to the caregiver but inaccessible to children. Have the diapering table close enough to the warm water supply so the water can be reached without leaving the child.

• Small, child-sized flush toilets are most appropriate; they are comfortable and sanitary for young children, especially toddlers who are just learning to use the toilet. Check that the toilet to be used by the child is clean and had been flushed after the previous child used it.

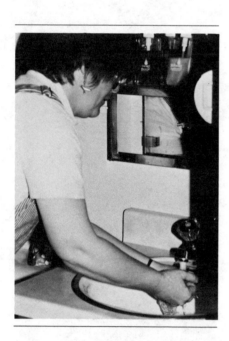

Feeding and Eating

• Bottles and eating utensils must be sanitized.

• Prepared formula, milk, and other perishable foods should be refrigerated at 40 degrees or colder.

• Bibs and other "burp" cloths need to be clean and fresh each time they are used.

• Clean feeding/eating tables with bleach solution after each use.

Napping and Resting

• Use separate storage for each child's bedding.

• Wash bedding (sheets, blankets) and wipe the mattress or mat with bleach every week or whenever soiled.

• Sick and contagious children should rest/nap in a separate area from the usual sleeping area.

• Distance each crib, cot, or mat from the other by at least one foot. More distance is even better and creates a less crowded feeling.

Guidelines for Detecting Illness

Caregivers should always be on the lookout for symptoms of illness. A quick check when the child arrives becomes an automatic response. Experienced caregivers are tuned in to recognize flushed faces, feverish eyes, and changes in breathing.

If the child arrives already ill, it is important to discover that fact before the parent leaves, unless the program has one of those rare facilities set up to take care of sick children. Parents may miss the symptoms themselves. They may lack knowledge about diseases in young children or they may have important reasons not to miss work and thus overlook or dismiss symptoms. The caregiver's job, if that should happen, is not to blame the parent but to be clear about what symptoms are apparent and to explain the policy on sickness. If the child's illness is severe enough or contagious, the caregiver must refuse to allow the child to stay.

When children or adults become *seriously ill* during the program, they need individual care and appropriate medical treatment. The common practice is to exclude ill children from a program or ask caregivers not to come to work until they are free from symptoms and are healthy enough to be active again in a group setting. When a caregiver becomes ill at work, the best policy is to leave work as soon as possible. In a family child care home it may be necessary to ask the parents to pick up their children early to allow the provider to take care of himself or herself. Excluding seriously ill adults and children from the program can help to prevent further spread of illness.

Mildly ill children do not generally pose a health threat to the other children or adults in the group. The main issue for caregivers is whether they can realistically care for mildly ill children and the other well children in the group at the same time. To gauge this reality, consider the severity of the child's illness, the type of illness, how the child is actually feeling, and the caregiver's or program's ability to care for the emotional and physical needs of a mildly ill child.

Whenever a child becomes ill, mildly or seriously, the parent(s) should be notified right away. Infections are most contagious before symptoms appear or when the symptoms first appear and the person starts feeling sick (shows signs of a sore throat, nausea, diarrhea, etc.). In most cases, once the symptoms are obvious, the group has already been exposed to the illness. Different illnesses have different exclusion criteria and waiting periods after treatment has begun. Exclusion policies need to be flexible and each child's illness needs to be judged individually, on a case-by-case basis.

Sick children must have their emotional needs attended to along with their physical needs. Caring for a mildly or seriously ill child in a group program usually means a balancing act for the caregiver(s). Sick children need a familiar adult to care for them and a quiet place to rest comfortably, away from the rest of the children.

Caregivers should always be on the lookout for symptoms of illness.

When a child becomes ill during the program, assess the severity of the symptom(s). If the symptoms cause discomfort and seem significant, make a careful check for all possible signs of illness.

Frequent Symptoms

Some of the symptoms that indicate possible disease or infection in infants and toddlers include:

Fever. The child may look flushed or pale and may be warm to the touch. (Your hand on the child's forehead may be deceiving if the hand itself is warm or cold.) When children become ill and show various symptoms, it is important to take their temperature.

The axillary or armpit method is best for taking the temperatures of infants and toddlers. *It is not safe or practical to use a mouth thermometer with young children.* Use a rectal thermometer (with a round, stubby bulb) and place the bulb securely in the child's armpit; hold the bulb in place for three minutes with the child's arm at his or her side. Temperatures taken by the armpit method are one degree lower than those taken orally and two degrees lower than those taken rectally. (*Note:* Fever strips are not reliable indicators of specific temperatures and are not recommended for determining accurate temperatures of young children.)

Unusual behavior. The normally placid child may be more active than usual. The "ball of energy" child may be listless. The usually happy child may be cranky. Crying for no apparent reason may also signal illness. Generally the child who "just is not himself or herself today" may be exhibiting symptoms of illness.

Changes in skin color or texture. The skin may look red, pale, or yellow. It may have unusual spots or rashes or it may itch.

Changes in the eyes. The whites of the eyes may be red or yellowish and tearing. The lids or the lining of the lids may be red or swollen. There may be discharge.

Respiratory difficulties. Problems may range from sniffles and a stuffy nose to coughing and wheezing. There may be either clear or colored discharge from the nose. Look for rapid breathing in the young infant. Changes in breathing rate may be the only indication that something is wrong.

Changes in stool. Diarrhea or loose stools can be either a symptom of another illness or an illness itself. Other changes, such as frequent bowel movements or pale or unusual colored stools, may be additional symptoms of disease. By keeping track of the consistency and

Exclusion policies need to be flexible and each child's illness needs to be judged individually, on a case-by-case basis.

frequency of the child's stools, you will be able to note anything unusual.

Changes in urine. Unusually dark, tea-colored urine is a warning sign. Infrequent, scanty urination may signal dehydration.

Changes in appetite. Sick children often do not eat well.

Vomiting. Hard to ignore, vomiting may or may not be a symptom of illness. Some babies spit up frequently; some toddlers throw up easily when they cough or gag. Vomiting is a symptom if it is unusual, either in amount or in frequency.

If the child has a fever of 101/102 (oral method), 100/101 (armpit method), 102/103 (rectal method), or higher or any symptoms that indicate the child is either infectious or too sick to be in child care, contact the parent(s) to have the child picked up as soon as possible.

To contact the parent(s), use the emergency form the parents filled out when they enrolled the child in the program (see sample form in the Appendix). Emergency forms need to include current home and work phone numbers of the parent(s); names, phone numbers, and relationship of at least two other people who are available to care for the child in case of emergency when the parents cannot be reached immediately; name, phone number, and address of the child's doctor/clinic; name of preferred hospital; insurance information; and signed permission for emergency treatment. When a child becomes sick or there is an emergency, reaching the parent(s) quickly is very important. Have the parent(s) check the information on the emergency form regularly to be sure the information is accurate. Let all parents know the importance of having correct emergency contact information and

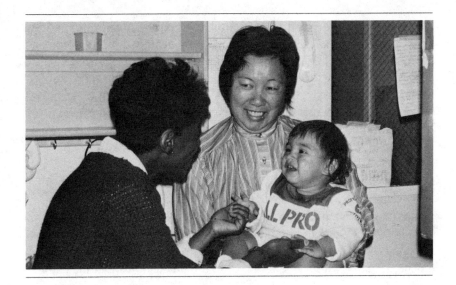

ask parents to update the information whenever the information changes.

When a child returns to the program, it is important that he or she feels well enough and has energy to participate fully in the group. Guidelines generally suggest that if a temperature has been 101/102 (oral method) or higher, it should be normal for at least 24 hours before the child returns to the program. Programs may also require a release from the child's doctor, especially for illnesses that are highly contagious.

Any medication to be given by the caregiver must be labeled by the pharmacist or the parent with the child's name, the drug's name, and the amount and times to be given. Parents should give written permission to administer all medications (see sample form in the Appendix).

Common Childhood Illnesses

Check with your county public health department and other medical references, such as the NAEYC publication *Healthy Young Children: A Manual for Programs,* for specific up-to-date treatment and exclusion guidelines for common childhood diseases. Some of the diseases you might expect to see in a program for infants and toddlers are described briefly below.

Allergies. Some allergies cause respiratory problems. Runny and stuffy noses can be caused by allergies. Severe allergy symptoms include coughing, congestion, wheezing, and difficulty in breathing. Other allergic symptoms may include diarrhea, vomiting, hives, and swelling. For serious allergies, parents have usually developed a plan with their family doctor in the event of a severe attack. This information, including all known allergies, should be available as part of the child's preadmission health history reported by parents.

Asthma. Occurring when bronchial tubes fill with mucous and go into spasm, asthma usually follows some allergy or infection. Symptoms are wheezing and difficulty in breathing. The chest often heaves trying to get air. A severe attack will result in blueness around the mouth and fingernails. Get immediate medical help if that happens. When asthma is recurring, parents have often developed a preventive medication plan with their family doctor to avert a severe attack. That is important information for caregivers to have.

Bronchitis. In children, bronchitis usually occurs in association with other conditions, such as a stuffy nose, the flu, or measles. The first symptom of bronchitis is a cough that develops gradually and is usually dry and hacking in nature. Occasionally the child may have a moderate fever. After one or two days the cough begins to produce mucus. Usually within five to ten days the mucus thins and the cough gradually disappears. Some children are a lot more susceptible to bronchitis than others.

Chicken pox. Chicken pox is the most widespread of the communicable childhood diseases (because a vaccine has not yet been developed). Infected children and adults must be excluded from the group. However, at the outset, when one is infectious, chicken pox symptoms are fever and crankiness, which make the disease difficult to distinguish from a host of other childhood diseases. Later, small bumps that look like flea bites will appear. In a day those bumps turn into weepy blisters, which dry and scab over in another day or two.

Colds. The cold is the most common health problem among young children. Cold symptoms include a cough, chest congestion, runny or plugged noses, with either clear or colored mucous, and perhaps watery eyes. Remember, however, those symptoms are often signs for allergies as well.

Croup. Viral croup occurs most frequently in children between the ages of three months and three years. The main symptom of croup is a peculiarly loud, harsh cough, which may or may not be accompanied by hoarseness and respiratory distress.

Ear infections. Usually following a cold or the flu, an ear infection has symptoms that include fussiness and excess crying, difficulty in sucking, difficulty in sleeping, and refusal to suck. Some children pull at the aching ear, but many do not. If the ear infection is severe, you may see discharge dried on or running out of the ear. All suspicious ear problems should be examined by the child's doctor. Untreated ear infections in young children sometimes lead to serious, permanent hearing loss.

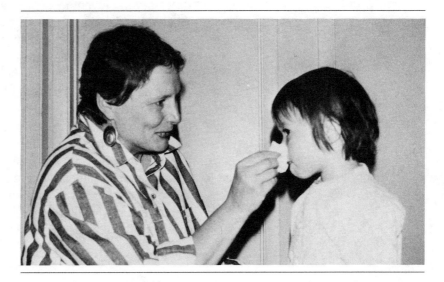

Flu. Flu is a very general term for virus-caused diseases that include symptoms of fever, aching muscles (probably not discernible in infants and toddlers), and general discomfort. Respiratory symptoms such as a runny or stuffy nose, coughing, and chest congestion may be present. Intestinal symptoms, including diarrhea, cramps, and vomiting, may also be present.

Giardia. Although many "bugs" can cause diarrhea, giardia deserves special attention. A common parasitic infection encountered in child care, giardia can cause severe diarrhea, especially in adults, and thus serious dehydration. Some children have no symptoms, others get by with just soft stools and vague abdominal complaints. But other children and adults get quite sick with intestinal upset, weakness, cramps, and severe diarrhea and dehydration. When giardia is suspected, the family doctor should be alerted and consulted for diagnosis and appropriate treatment.

Hepatitis A. Hepatitis A is usually a mild disease in young children but can spread rapidly throughout the program, causing more severe illness in caregivers. The typical symptoms of hepatitis, yellowish cast to the skin and whites of the eyes, show up in only half the infected children under two years of age. Other symptoms look like the stomach flu. Hepatitis A is spread through infected fecal matter.

Lice. Although lice do not transmit diseases, they are very annoying and easily spread through person-to-person contact. The major symptom is itching. Usually nits (small transparent eggs) can be seen attached to the base of the hair. A prescription shampoo treatment kills the nits. Fairly elaborate and persistent precautions must be taken by parents at home as well as the program staff. In addition to checking all children regularly after an outbreak of lice, special cleaning is necessary to prevent recurring cases of lice. This includes laundering all clothing, bedding, pillows, stuffed animals, and common play clothes, especially hats; cleaning couches and carpets; and disinfecting all hairbrushes and combs.

Shigella. Shigella is a bacterial infection that may cause mild to severe diarrhea, vomiting, fever, severe cramps, and convulsions. (Severe diarrhea may result in serious dehydration.) Improper handwashing after changing children's diapers is one of the main ways this infection may be spread in group care situations. Even though shigella is most common among young children, adults may also be affected. When a child or staff member is diagnosed with shigella, other parents and staff should be notified so that the family doctor may be consulted for diagnosis and treatment.

Strep throat. Strep throat occurs mostly in children more than a year old. Symptoms include sore throat, fever, and swollen glands in the neck.

Thrush. A yeast infection occurring mostly in young infants, thrush can cause diaper rash as well as sores in the mouth. The symptoms are a diaper rash that will not clear up and "milk curds" in the mouth over the gums, the tongue, and inside the cheeks. Babies with thrush may be fussy but not very sick.

Tonsillitis. Tonsils can become infected by either viruses or bacteria. Tonsillitis often follows a cold or other illness. Symptoms include fever (often high) and a sore throat. Glands in the neck are sometimes swollen.

Severe Infectious Diseases

Caring for infants and toddlers requires special precautions against infectious diseases. The very young child's inability to control bodily fluids and secretions (urine, fecal matter, mucous, blood, and saliva) increases the potential for the spread of infectious diseases. Therefore, it is important that caregivers familiarize themselves with disease prevention.

In addition to *careful, consistent handwashing,* discussed earlier in this section, *immunizations* for the adults as well as for the children are an important and effective means of preventing some infectious diseases or preventing further spread of those diseases among the children and adults in the child care setting. For example, effective vaccines are available for the prevention of polio, diphtheria, tetanus, mumps, measles, and rubella. According to *Healthy Young Children: A Manual for Programs,* "These vaccines are strongly recommended for employees," and also a "vaccine for influenza virus (given yearly) may be advisable" (p. 137).[1]

The manual continues: "Unborn children can acquire several infectious diseases. Such infections can cause miscarriage, birth defects, or illness in the newborn. These infections include rubella, measles, mumps, hepatitis B, cytomegalovirus, herpes, and AIDS. The first four diseases can be prevented by immunization. Routine immunization (or other proof of immunity) is strongly recommended for the first three diseases: measles, mumps, and rubella. In certain settings, an increased risk of hepatitis B infection could exist. In those cases, vaccination is recommended for persons who have daily close contact with children who have or are at high risk of having hepatitis B. Strict attention to handwashing and care with all children's blood

Urine, fecal matter, mucous, blood, and saliva should all be considered potentially infectious substances.

---

[1]*Healthy Young Children: A Manual for Programs.* Edited by Abby Shapiro Kendrick and others. Copyright © 1988 by the National Association for the Education of Young Children. Excerpts used by permission.

and body fluids are the most effective safeguards for susceptible women [of childbearing age] against those infections for which there are no vaccines." (*Healthy Young Children,* p. 140)

Herpes simplex and AIDS/HIV infections pose special concerns for programs for infants and toddlers. Care and consideration help children with those particular diseases to lead as normal a life as possible while they are ill. Sensitive and well-informed caregivers can provide important support to the ill child's family and all families in the program during the period of illness.

Because of the complexity of herpes simplex and AIDS/HIV infections and the fact that information about them and their prevention is developing so rapidly, caregivers should refer to the resource material cited in the reference section and the public health/medical agencies in their community for current, updated information. However, to provide basic information, excerpts from *Healthy Young Children: A Manual for Programs* are included below:

"*Herpes simplex viral* (HSV) infections are characterized by skin blisters or sores that can be very painful. Once a person is infected these viruses remain in nerve cells, and HSV tends to recur at the same places on the body again and again. There are two types of herpes virus—HSV type 1 (usually found in the mouth) and HSV type 2 (usually found on the genitals)." (*Healthy Young Children,* p. 265)

"Exclude children or staff with open, oozing sores that cannot be covered. Exclude all cases of herpetic whitlow [herpetic sores on fingers] if the sores are not crusted. Do not allow staff with oral (mouth) blisters to care for children (since close physical contact might spread HSV). . . . *Do not exclude* children or staff with skin blisters (in locations other than the mouth or finger) that can be covered or with genital herpes. . . . Make sure that staff who may touch blisters on children wear [surgical] gloves during diapering or changing of a dressing." (*Healthy Young Children,* p. 266)

"*Hepatitis B* is a viral infection of the liver. Symptoms of infection include fever, loss of appetite, nausea, jaundice (yellowing of the skin and whites of the eyes), and occasionally pain of the joints and a hivelike skin rash. Illness can range from infection without symptoms to the very rare event of rapid liver failure and death. . . . Hepatitis B is transmitted when blood or body fluids containing the virus get onto skin or mucosal surfaces (inside the mouth, eyes, rectum, or genital tract)." (*Healthy Young Children,* p. 267)

"A staff person ill with hepatitis B should stay home until she or he feels well and fever and jaundice are gone. A staff person with chronic hepatitis B infection who has open, oozing sores that cannot be covered should not attend until the skin sores are healed." (*Healthy Young Children,* p. 269)

Excluding infants and toddlers with hepatitis B may be necessary, or at least "a more restrictive environment may be desired for those children, because they . . . lack control of their body secretions, share items contaminated with secretions, and/or display behavior (e.g., being bitten) that may raise the risk of virus transmission." (*Healthy Young Children*, p. 269)

"AIDS/HIV infections. HIV (human immunodeficiency virus) infections which include AIDS (Acquired Immune Deficiency Syndrome) and ARC (AIDS-related complex) are very serious viral infections. . . . AIDS is a disease that leaves an individual vulnerable to illnesses that a healthy immune system might otherwise overcome. It is caused by a virus, human immunodeficiency virus (HIV). . . . Studies show that AIDS is transmitted primarily via intimate sexual contact, blood-to-blood contact, or from an infected mother to her baby. . . . However, the risk of transmission of HIV *among preschool children and the developmentally disabled in a group setting* raises special *theoretical* considerations that are not relevant in older children or with adults. Because children in the birth through 3 years age group and the developmentally disabled may lack control of their bodily secretions or may display behavior such as biting, it may be necessary to require a more restrictive environment for these children until more is known about transmission of AIDS/HIV in these group settings. . . . Children from birth through age 3 years who have clinical AIDS *should not attend a group setting* because of their increased susceptibility to infection." (*Healthy Young Children*, p. 270)

Other recommendations from the NAEYC publication indicate that restrictions for preschool children aged four and five years are not generally necessary. However, specific limitations may be required if certain conditions (medical or behavioral) exist—conditions such as open sores and skin eruptions that cannot be covered or the likelihood of biting behavior by the infected child or his or her peers. "In either of these cases, the child's physician and the program should collaborate to decide about the appropriateness of the child's attendance." (*Healthy Young Children*, p. 271)

Cytomegalovirus (CMV) is known to cause birth defects if contracted during pregnancy. Therefore, CMV is of serious concern to pregnant women, especially in the first trimester, and to women of childbearing age anticipating pregnancy.

However, CMV is a very common infection, often asymptomatic (no apparent symptoms) among young children. The disease does not generally affect children seriously, and children are not to be excluded from care unless they are sick and show symptoms of the illness. The concern regarding CMV is for pregnant women or women trying to become pregnant, because CMV is known to cause birth defects

including "mental retardation, hearing loss, or other sensoric problems." (*Healthy Young Children*, p. 265)

Anyone in the program who has been exposed to a *communicable disease* (that is, children's parents and program staff) should be notified about the exposure. A standard *exposure notice* should be posted which indicates: (1) the occurrence of the particular illness; (2) the contagion period; (3) the exposure circumstances; and (4) pertinent information about the illness. (Sample forms are included in the Appendix.) Check with your local health department for diseases that should be reported to it and the particular circumstances under which the department's guidelines apply.

Guidelines for a Safe Environment

As the timeless adage goes, "an ounce of prevention is worth a pound of cure." Nothing could be more appropriate to the care of young children. Every month in the United States, 400 children under the age of four die in accidents, reports the American Academy of Pediatrics. Most of these accidents could have been prevented. As a caregiver you need to be knowledgeable about basic, up-to-date methods of first aid and CPR (cardiopulmonary resuscitation) for children.

A first aid course, taken every couple of years, will give you confidence to decide when an injury is minor enough for you to handle on your own and when to call for help. Most injuries that you encounter will be minor and can be handled with the materials from a first aid kit. A yearly course in CPR for children will prepare you to handle cardiopulmonary resuscitation emergencies.

Common minor injuries that need attention in infant/toddler child care are bumps, scratches, bites (human and insect), and stings. Burns, cuts, and poisoning can also occur but they are preventable by careful monitoring of the environment and consistent safety measures. Less preventable, and with the potential for serious consequences, are respiratory emergencies caused by a variety of sources—allergies, asthma, swallowed objects, aspirated substances and objects—and, in young infants, immature nervous systems.

Preventing Accidents and Injuries

Preventive measures can be taken to reduce the risk of accidents and injury. Suggestions are listed below for each of the routine areas of diapering, toileting, and bathing; feeding and eating; and resting and napping:

Diapering, toileting, and bathing. Never leave a child alone during diapering, bathing, or toileting routines. Be sure to have all your necessary supplies close at hand, including warm water for washing.

Be sure that the warm water temperature at the water heater is not above 110°F. Test the water for washing and bathing before allowing the water to touch the child.

When bathing a child, be sure there is a nonskid mat or strip in the tub to prevent slipping.

Feeding and eating. Ask parents to provide you with information on the child's allergic reaction to any foods as part of the medical history parents provide when they enroll the child. Post the information for each child in the group in the food preparation/eating area so it is

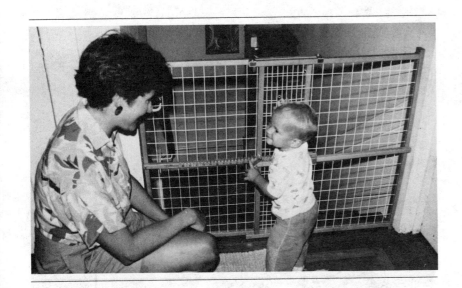

Most accidents can be prevented.

available for careful monitoring and a quick reference *before* any foods are given to the child.

Be sure to feed children appropriate foods. Infants and toddlers can easily aspirate or choke on foods that have a hard, crunchy texture and on some soft foods as well. Common foods to avoid include carrot sticks, apple slices, hot dog rounds, marshmallows, peanut butter, grapes, popcorn, raisins, peanuts, and other nuts.

Infants should always be held for bottle nursing; they should not have bottles alone in their cribs, on pillows, or walking around. Children can choke easily on liquids from a bottle when they are not supervised. Also nursing on a bottle for a long time in a crib or on a pillow can cause serious tooth decay and chronic ear infection.

High chairs are convenient for adults but may be unsafe for the mobile, active child who tries to climb in or out. Consider holding infants while feeding them until they can sit alone. When children are able to sit by themselves and can crawl in and out of a low seat, that type of seating is preferable. Low, child-sized seats, like Educubes, placed on the floor around a low table provide the young mobile child safety, independence, and a social experience at mealtimes. Round tables are best because there are no corners for children to bump into.

Glass should not be used for children's bottles, cups, or dishes for safety reasons. Plastic is most appropriate, and clear plastic is helpful for children's bottles and drinking glasses so both you and the child can see the liquid.

Resting and napping. All cribs should be child-proofed before they are used. Inspect the crib or cot to be sure there are no gaps between the mattress and the sides where arms and legs might get caught. The minimum rail height should be 22 inches from the top of the railing to the mattress when the rail is set at the lowest level. Slat spacing

should be no more than 2 3/8 inches apart. Wood surfaces should be free of splinters and cracks and have lead-free paint. The sides should be at least 4 inches above the mattress when in the lowered position and should not have cross bars, so the child can neither fall nor climb out.

Be sure there are no objects in the crib on which the child could choke or that could smother the child. Stringed objects in or around the crib, such as hanging drapery cords, or objects strung over the crib can cause strangulation. Objects on which the child might stand and thus climb and fall out of the crib are hazards, too.

When you move a mobile infant from sleeping or resting in a crib to a low cot or mat, you promote autonomy and independence. You also prevent accidents resulting from climbing and falling out of the crib. Like a high chair, a high crib is convenient for the adult but may pose a safety hazard for a child who can climb out. Low sleeping cribs, cots, or mats are preferable for older infants or toddlers.

Preparing for Injuries

A well-stocked first aid kit is the primary preparation for treating injuries. You can buy one or make up your own. Keep the kit in the same location and make the kit portable so it can be taken to the scene of the accident in case the injured person cannot be moved. Replenish supplies so the kit is always fully stocked. The following supplies should be included in your kit:

- Thermometers (rectal type to be used for axillary/armpit temperature)
- Tweezers
- Absorbent cotton
- Adhesive tape
- Adhesive strip bandages
- Sterile gauze bandages (assorted sizes to fit the infant/toddler)
- Sterile gauze pads
- Children's acetaminophen, such as Tylenol (do not give medication without written permission from the child's parents)
- Cotton-tipped swabs
- Rubbing alcohol
- Drinking cups
- Measuring spoon
- Safety pins
- Sharp scissors
- Tongue depressors

- Syrup of Ipecac (to induce vomiting—if instructed to do so by the poison control center)
- Activated charcoal (to absorb poison—if instructed to do so by the poison control center)
- Epsom salts (a laxative—to use only if instructed to do so by the poison control center)

Accidents and injury to both staff and children need to be taken care of immediately. When a child is injured, you should quickly and carefully assess the situation and decide whether the child should or should not be moved from the site of the accident. *Serious damage can be done to someone if he or she is moved when bones are broken or there are internal injuries.*

You also need to decide quickly if the injury is life-threatening, in which case you should call the paramedics immediately (dial 911 in most areas or O for the operator). Phone numbers for paramedics, fire, police, available adults who will come immediately to help, and the emergency information for children's parents must be clearly posted and accessible at the telephone for use in case of emergency.

It is important to develop a plan ahead of time for getting additional adult help immediately when an emergency occurs. In center-based programs the plan should designate how you will let other staff know you need help to care for the other children in the group and who will call the hurt or ill child's parents. This procedure will allow the primary caregiver to care for the child as long as possible. Family child care providers should have plans to obtain assistance from a nearby neighbor if necessary.

You also need to be aware that one child's injury or illness will have an impact on the other children in the group. Although you are busy, it is important that you do not ignore the rest of the children.

It is important to develop a plan ahead of time for getting additional adult help immediately when an emergency occurs.

Children in the group will respond to the situation in their own unique manner. For instance, one child may become distressed, another may seem unfazed, and still another may not notice at all. Do what you can to calm and reassure each and every child in the group, including the injured child. Explain to the children, in simple terms and a matter-of-fact way, what is happening.

As in most other aspects of caregiving, you are being asked again to perform a balancing act. If the emergency is great enough, you will focus, of course, on the injured child. The other children may have to wait for your calm attention until the emergency is over—though some children, because of their own distress, may act out in ways that demand attention during the emergency. While you are busy and distracted with an injured or ill child, other accidents often occur. Instruct your helping adults to be especially attentive, calm, and reassuring with the children while you attend to the emergency.

Remember that any unusual event in the program affects all the children and adults. Do not just drop the subject after the emergency is over. Instead, encourage the children who can talk to express their feelings; allow crying as an expression of feelings also. Be as comforting as you can while you acknowledge what the children are feeling.

Keeping Records of Injuries

Any time an injury to a child occurs, an accident report must be filled out. A written report provides the parent with a record of the important details, and even minor accidents will not go unnoticed or be forgotten. The person who observed the incident should fill out the report as soon as possible after the injury. In particular, note the date, time, what happened, what action was taken and by whom. An accident report form is included in the Appendix. Check with state or local licensing agencies to see if there are reporting requirements for accidents in your area.

Notifying Parents

Whenever a child has an accident that requires medical attention beyond minor first aid for a scrape or small bump, you should notify the parents right away. Parents should also be notified immediately of any injuries to the head or accidents, such as falls, which may have caused internal injuries, even when the child seems to recover quickly.

Guidelines for Emergency Drill Procedures

Monthly drills to ensure emergency preparedness may be required by state or local licensing agencies. Even if there are no requirements for regular drills, caregivers are responsible for developing a detailed procedure for fire and earthquake and other disasters. The procedures should be part of the orientation of all new staff members and parents. In addition, both parents and staff need to make disaster plans for their own families, and that information needs to be discussed and incorporated, when feasible, into the child care program's plan. For example, in case of an earthquake, which parent will try to reach the child in child care? How are staff members with children prepared to cope with the needs of the child care program and those of their own family?

Periodically during the year the procedures should be reviewed with all staff and in group parent and staff meetings. Check with local agencies for emergency drill procedures for different types of disasters that may occur in your area.

Listed below are some basic guidelines for fire and earthquake drill procedures.

Fire Drills

The same person should schedule and conduct a fire drill once a month. When the alarm sounds, immediately evacuate all the children: carry infants or place them in a crib and push them to the holding area away from the building; walk or carry toddlers to the holding area. Take the attendance of all children and adults before anyone returns to the building. Document the time necessary to evacuate the building for each drill. All caregivers should critique the procedure for future improvement.

The same person should schedule and conduct a fire drill once a month.

In case of a real fire, anyone on the premises who notices the fire should sound the alarm and call the local fire department (remember this emergency phone number is to be posted by each telephone). For some buildings it is possible for the alarm to register at the local fire department. Evacuate children to the holding areas and hold them there until the building is cleared by the fire department. Take attendance for all children and adults before anyone returns to the building. If necessary, notify parents to come and pick up their children. In any event, parents should be informed about the fire and its possible impact on the children.

Earthquake Drills

Earthquake drills also need to be conducted on a regular basis. The children who are older and can understand should be taught to "duck and cover" in the room they are in, crawling under tables and away from windows and other glass. Practice this procedure every month in a matter-of-fact way with the children, both inside and out-of-doors. During the practice drills, explain *in very simple terms* that if there were an earthquake the floor or ground would shake. In order to be safe from falling debris, everyone must "duck and cover," getting under the tables when inside the building or to an open space out-of-doors. The open space outside should be away from power lines or poles, trees, glass, high structures that might fall, and the like.

When infants are inside, you should gather them together away from mirrors, windows, and other glass. Loose, large pillows can be used to corral the children. If possible, gather the infants in a spot that offers protection from falling debris. Outside, gather the infants around you in an open space, away from power lines or poles, trees, glass, high structures that might fall, and so on.

When making disaster plans, be sure the plans are safe and practical to use with the children. Any adults who are part of the program but not directly responsible for children must know they are essential during a disaster and will be needed to assist with all of the children and adults for the entire program. The assignment of those adults should be part of the disaster preparedness plan. Arranging for the availability of parents and extra helping adults should also be part of the plan.

When making disaster plans, be sure the plans are safe and practical to use with the children.

Emergency kits that have flashlights and other emergency supplies, including a cache of food, additional first aid supplies, water, blankets, extra clothing, and diapers, should be set up in an area or areas most likely to be accessible and undamaged in the event of a real earthquake.

If a real earthquake occurs, children and adults should take cover wherever they are at the time of the quake. If children are inside, they should remain inside, but they should be moved quickly outside as soon as it is safe to do so. You should hold the children in the outside holding area until you determine it is safe to return to the building. Take the attendance of all children and adults before anyone returns to the building. The disaster plan should include arrangements for notifying parents when it is necessary to come and pick up their children. Arrangements should also include plans to care for the children until the parents are able to pick them up.

Points to Consider

1. Do you have clearly written health and safety policies and guidelines for your program? Do you give copies of the policies and guidelines to your parents when they enroll their child(ren) in your program and do you go over the guidelines during the parent orientation to your program?

2. Do you have located adjacent to your phone up-to-date emergency information and signed releases for all of your children as well as emergency phone numbers for paramedics, fire, police, poison control, and available helping adults?

3. Do you know how to maintain a safe and healthy environment and how to prevent illnesses and accidents whenever possible?

4. Have you child-proofed your environment from the child's view-

point (get down on your hands and knees to get the real perspective) for safety and health while still providing an enriched environment that says "yes" to the child to explore and be curious?

5. Do you and the other caregivers know how to respond to various symptoms of illness and how to give first aid in case of injury? Do you have a completely stocked first aid kit and emergency supplies on hand in case of emergency?

6. Do you have plans or ideas about how to maintain a calm social–emotional climate during times of illness and injury?

Suggested Resources

Books and Articles

American Academy of Pediatrics, Committee on Accident and Poison Prevention. *Handbook of Common Poisonings in Children* (Second edition). Elk Grove Village, Ill.: The American Academy of Pediatrics, 1983.

American Academy of Pediatrics, Committee on Early Childhood, Adoption and Dependent Care. *Health Day Care: A Manual for Health Professionals.* Elk Grove Village, Ill.: The American Academy of Pediatrics, 1987.

Green, Martin I. *A Sigh of Relief: First-Aid Handbook for Childhood Emergencies* (Revised edition). New York: Bantam Books, Inc., 1984.

Contains fast, simple instructions for childhood injuries and illnesses.

Healthy Young Children: A Manual for Programs. Edited by Abby Shapiro Kendrick and others. Washington, D.C.: National Association for the Education of Young Children, 1988. Available from NAEYC, 1834 Connecticut Ave., N.W., Washington, DC 20009-5786.

Infant and Toddler Program Quality Review Instrument. Sacramento: California State Department of Education, 1988.

Provides guidelines for assessing the quality of programs for infants and toddlers.

Injury Control for Children and Youth 1987. Edited by the American Academy of Pediatrics, Committee on Accident and Poison Prevention. Elk Grove Village, Ill.: The American Academy of Pediatrics, 1987.

Moukaddem, V. "Preventing Infectious Diseases in Your Child Care Setting," *Young Children,* Vol. 45 (1990), 28–29.

Presents information about infectious diseases and how to control them in a child care environment.

Nash, M., and C. Tate. "Health, Safety and First Aid," in *Better Baby Care: A Book for Family Day Care Providers*. Washington, D.C.: The Children's Foundation, 1986, pp. 87–103.

Offers sound advice and suggestions on how to handle health and safety concerns with infants and toddlers in family child care. Also useful for center-based caregivers.

Smith, Lendon. *The Encyclopedia of Baby and Child Care* (Revised edition). Englewood Cliffs, N.J.: Prentice Hall, 1981.

Contains information about emergencies, first aid, poisonings, fevers, and allergies—as well as what you need to know about anatomy and development of infants and toddlers.

Standard First Aid and Personal Safety. Prepared by the American Red Cross. Fort Wayne, Ind.: American Red Cross, Allen-Wells Chapter, 1987.

Deals with a wide variety of specific injuries and emergency situations.

Visions for Infant/Toddler Care: Guidelines for Professional Caregiving. Sacramento: California State Department of Education, 1988.

Presents goals or visions for quality care of infants and toddlers, which should be considered by caregivers and directors of child care.

Willis, Anne, and Henry Ricciuti. *A Good Beginning for Babies: Guidelines for Group Care*. Washington, D.C.: National Association for the Education of Young Children, 1975.

Contains a chapter on health and safety as well as a list of symptoms and a sample letter for parents regarding illness.

Audiovisuals

A Good Measure of Safety. A program in "Spoonful of Lovin'." Bloomington, Ind. Agency for Instructional Television, [n.d.]. Videocassette, 30 minutes.

Presents information on safety for young children. Encourages caregivers to look at the environment from the child's eye level in order to be more aware of dangers. Identifies common substances that can be poisonous for young children. Explains first aid procedures for bleeding, breathing trouble, and poison. Available from Agency for Instructional Television, Box A, Bloomington, IN 47402.

Healthy Child Care: Is It Really Magic? San Francisco: Insight Productions, 1988. Videocassette.

For further information regarding distribution and purchase, contact: Bananas, 6501 Telegraph Avenue, Oakland, CA 94609.

Infant Health Care: A First Year Support Guide for New Parents. Johnson and Johnson Parenting Video.

Call toll-free 1-800-537-2336 for further information.

It's Not Just Routine: Feeding, Diapering, and Napping Infants and Toddlers. Sacramento: California State Department of Education, 1990. Videocassette, color, 24 minutes; printed guide.

Illustrates health and safety concerns in the caregiving routines of feeding, diapering, and napping.

Space to Grow: Creating a Child Care Environment for Infants and Toddlers. Sacramento: California State Department of Education, 1988. Videocassette, color, 22 minutes; printed guide.

Presents eight concepts, including health and safety, to consider in setting up environments for infants and toddlers.

Section Eight: Recordkeeping

Caregivers must keep a number of records. This section deals with those that pertain directly to individual children and their families and concentrates on the records that make up a developmental profile. Daily records of the various caregiving activities have been discussed in other chapters and will not be repeated here, but those records may also be part of the developmental profile.

One purpose of keeping records is to build a picture of each child's development so that caregivers can plan individualized programs. The picture includes the child's range of general and specific needs at the present time and the family's expectations. By looking at the individual picture, caregivers can plan a program to respond to each participant.

The Importance of Written Records

Sometimes caregivers resist keeping written records of individual development. Experienced caregivers assess development informally every day because they know each child, what he or she can do, and what he or she cannot do. Even beginning caregivers usually can see growth and development quite easily, but written records are still

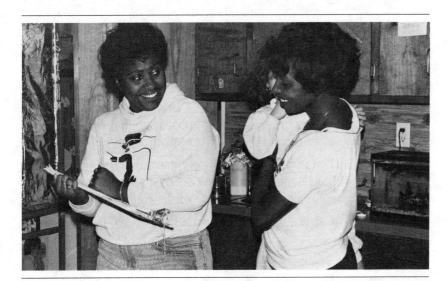

One purpose of keeping records is to build a picture of each child's development so that you can plan individualized programs.

Each child's development is individual. No child is average.

important. Often caregivers' memories play tricks on them. Without written records patterns are harder to see.

Most of the time development is normal, and no one need worry about it. Sometimes, however, patterns of developmental lags become evident, and the child may need more than the carefully planned individualized program is able to provide. Experienced caregivers notice the lags without formal training in developmental assessment. Beginning caregivers can determine what is normal by comparing individual developmental checklists to standardized developmental charts.

A word of caution—be very careful about comparing one child to another or using the chart to determine anything but pronounced developmental lags. Do not use the chart to write report cards. Each child's development is individual. No child is average. If you begin to label children "advanced" or "average" or "slow" at this tender age, you do them and their parents a grave disservice. The notion of *self-fulfilling prophecy,* in which expectations influence the outcome, is a fact. Do not let a label influence a child's future. Developmental profiles do not predict future success or failure in either school specifically or life in general. The exception is at either extreme of the scale. If the child's development is extreme, you will notice it without needing a developmental chart.

Sources of Information

Two ways to gather information are through forms and interviews. The information should include the following:

1. Developmental history, including at what age the child reached major milestones (rolled over, started to walk, etc.) plus individual information, such as words for bodily functions, fears, favorite toys, and the like.

2. Health history, including special prenatal and birth circumstances, chronic health conditions, food allergies, medication needed, and so on.

3. Nutrition information, such as type of formula, introduction of solid foods, and food preferences.

4. Child-rearing practices, including types of guidance and family expectations for the child.

5. Family background, including family makeup, family members, ages of siblings, language spoken in the home, cultural values, parental preferences regarding care of the child, and so forth.

6. Special considerations, such as social services requests and so on.

Sample forms provided in the Appendix indicate how some of the information can be organized. For example:

- "Physician's Report—Day Care Center." A preadmission health evaluation by a physician is a licensing requirement and provides an expert opinion on the child's health and health history. Sometimes a medical condition can give clues to developmental patterns. For example, a baby with a history of ear infections needs to be watched for signs of temporary hearing loss, which can result in delayed language development.

- "Child's Preadmission Health History—Parent's Report." A preadmission health history reported by the parent is also helpful in evaluating development. The sample form from the California State Department of Social Services is fairly simple and general. The extended version goes beyond a simple health history and looks at daily routines, habits, the parent's evaluation of the child's personality, and special problems—likes and dislikes, fears, and so on.

- "Medication Release." The form is to be used if the child needs medication while he or she is in child care.

- "Infant Diet/Meal Plan." The form ensures that parents and caregivers share the same knowledge about which solid foods already have been introduced, the type of formula used, whether or not the baby is breast-fed, and the schedule for introducing new foods.

In addition to the forms, caregivers' notes based on knowledge of and interviews with the family round out the file. Information may come from informal daily contacts but should also come from planned, formal parent conferences held at regular intervals. The child's growth and development should be the focus of the conferences.

Each child's file should contain specific up-to-date information on the child's development in each of the following areas:

1. Social-emotional development

2. Physical development

3. Language development

4. Cognitive development

The sample checklist included at the end of this section can be used regularly to assess each child's development in each area. By keeping such records, you can chart specific progress in each developmental area.

Be sure that all records remain confidential. This sort of information is not to be passed around. Records should be in locked file cabinets, not available to other parents or visitors.

Profile of Infant Development: Sample Checklist

Name: _____ Birth Date: _____

Social–Emotional Development

Young Infant (to about nine months)   *Date Observed*
Makes eye contact   _____
Smiles back at adults   _____
Recognizes primary caregiver   _____
Laughs at patty-cake and peek-a-boo games   _____
Withdraws or cries when stranger approaches   _____
Shows dislike when familiar toy is removed   _____
Other   _____

Mobile Infant (to about eighteen months)   *Date Observed*
Shows discomfort on separation from mother   _____
Participates in peek-a-boo and patty-cake games   _____
Offers and gives toy to adult   _____
Knows difference between own possession and others'   _____
Initiates social games like ball play   _____
Other   _____

Toddler (to about thirty-six months)   *Date Observed*
Protests when activity is blocked   _____
Picks up and puts away toys on request   _____
Shows affection—carries or hugs doll, shows regard
    for people or possessions   _____
Occupies self, thinks up own play activities, or acts on
    simple suggestions   _____
Explores, investigates surroundings   _____
Plays alone but alongside or among other children,
    focuses on own activity but is aware of theirs
    without disturbing them   _____
Plays and interacts with other children   _____
Helps at little tasks   _____
Other   _____

Physical—Large-muscle Development

Young Infant (to about nine months)   *Date Observed*
Controls head   _____
Rolls from back to side   _____
Rolls from back to front   _____
Creeps or inches forward or backward   _____
Other   _____

Mobile Infant (to about eighteen months)   *Date Observed*
Crawls   _____
Gets into sitting position   _____
Pulls to stand   _____
Cruises holding onto furniture   _____
Walks independently   _____
Other   _____

Toddler (to about thirty-six months)   *Date Observed*
Walks fast and well   _____
Runs awkwardly   _____
Walks up stairs holding a hand   _____
Walks backward   _____
Climbs   _____
Runs well   _____
Throws ball with aim   _____
Walks up stairs without a hand   _____
Jumps   _____
Can stand on one foot briefly   _____
Other   _____

Physical—Small-muscle Development

Young Infant (to about nine months)   *Date Observed*
Coordinates sucking, swallowing, and breathing   _____
Gums and swallows textured foods   _____
Drinks from cup with help   _____
Closes lips on spoon to remove food   _____
Picks up spoon   _____
Reaches for and grabs toy   _____
Transfers toy from hand to hand   _____
Other   _____

Mobile Infant (to about eighteen months)   *Date Observed*
Feeds self small bits of food using fingers   _____
Eats cracker   _____
Eats mashed table foods   _____
Uses thumb and forefinger to pick up small items   _____
Turns pages of books   _____
Scribbles   _____
Other   _____

Toddler (to about thirty-six months)   *Date Observed*
Drinks from cup unassisted   _____
Feeds self well using spoon   _____
Washes and dries hands alone   _____
Unfastens clothing   _____

Removes simple garments   _____
Exercises bladder and bowel control   _____
Cares for self at toilet   _____
Puts coat and shoes on   _____
Stacks blocks   _____
Puts pegs in pegboard   _____
Takes covers from objects   _____
Takes things apart   _____
Puts things together (like simple construction toys)   _____
Uses paint brush   _____
Other   _____

Language Development

Young Infant (to about nine months)   *Date Observed*
Turns head in direction of voices and sounds   _____
Listens   _____
Cries   _____
Responds to voices   _____
Coos, whimpers, gurgles, and makes a variety of sounds   _____
"Talks" to self and others   _____
Imitates sounds   _____
Other   _____

Mobile Infant (to about eighteen months)   *Date Observed*
Knows that words stand for objects   _____
Responds to words   _____
Carries out simple commands   _____
Expresses self using gestures and movements   _____
Uses words such as "mama"   _____
Has intonation   _____
Other   _____

Toddler (to about thirty-six months)   *Date Observed*
Shows body parts, clothing items, or toys on request   _____
Labels objects   _____
Follows two simple directions   _____
Uses two-word sentences   _____
Uses name when referring to self   _____
Names pictures in a book   _____
Listens to stories or rhymes   _____
Uses personal pronouns I, me, you   _____
Converses in short sentences   _____
Answers questions   _____
Uses language to convey ideas   _____
Has fairly clear pronunciation   _____
Other   _____

Cognitive Development

Young Infant (to about nine months)	*Date Observed*
Is visually alert a good part of waking hours	_____
Recognizes familiar objects	_____
Looks for dropped objects	_____
Is able to use several senses at once	_____
Is able to remember games and toys from previous days	_____
Anticipates return of people	_____
Is able to concentrate	_____
Pulls cover off toy when hidden	_____
Solves simple manipulative problems	_____
Shows interest in discovering the consequences of own behavior	_____
Other	_____

Mobile Infant (to about eighteen months)	*Date Observed*
Is good at finding hidden objects	_____
Uses trial-and-error method effectively	_____
Explores new approaches to problems	_____
Thinks about actions before doing them	_____
Imitates people who are not present	_____
Other	_____

Toddler (to about thirty-six months)	*Date Observed*
Fantasizes and role plays	_____
Memorizes phrases of songs	_____
Identifies pictures of common objects	_____
Works simple puzzles	_____
Counts to two or three	_____
Knows he is a boy or she is a girl	_____
Knows most of the body parts	_____
Compares sizes, shapes, colors	_____
Names actions in pictures	_____
Uses plurals	_____
Expresses self using words	_____
Other	_____

Points to Consider

1. How well do the records you keep provide a developmental profile of each child in your care? In what ways can you improve your recordkeeping?

2. In what ways do you use the developmental profile you have of each child (either in your head or on paper) to make daily, weekly, monthly plans? (Consider the ways in which you set up the environment, plan for materials and activities, plan approaches in dealing with behaviors, make changes in caregiving routines.)

3. In what ways do you plan for the enhancement of the social–emotional, physical, language, and cognitive development of each child in your care?

Suggested Resources

Beaty, Janice J. *Observing Development of the Preschool Child.* Columbus, Ohio: Merrill Publishing Co., 1986.

Focuses on the child two to six years of age. Presents a system of observing and recording development in six areas: emotional, social, motor, cognitive, language, and creative.

Cohen, Dorothy H., and Virginia Stern. *Observing and Recording the Behavior of Young Children* (Third, revised edition). New York: Columbia University, Teachers College, Teachers College Press, 1983.

Focuses mostly on preschool age but includes a chapter on observing infants and toddlers.

Developmentally Appropriate Practice in Early Childhood Programs Serving Children from Birth to Age 8. Edited by Sue Bredekamp. Washington, D.C.: National Association for the Education of Young Children, 1986.

Part Two contains guidelines and information on how infants and toddlers develop.

The First Twelve Months of Life. Edited by Frank Caplan. New York: Bantam Books, Inc., 1984.

Describes growth and development month by month and contains 12 growth charts as well as several photographs.

Infant and Toddler Program Quality Review Instrument. Sacramento: California State Department of Education, 1988.

Provides guidelines for assessing the quality of programs for infants and toddlers.

The Second Twelve Months of Life. Edited by Frank Caplan. New York: Bantam Books, Inc., 1982.

Describes growth and development during the second year of life.

Visions for Infant/Toddler Care: Guidelines for Professional Caregiving. Sacramento: California State Department of Education, 1988.

Presents goals or visions for quality care of infants and toddlers, which should be considered by caregivers and directors of child care.

Section Nine: Special Issues with Children and Families

In the United States there are families from many different countries of origin, representing a wide variety of religious, ethnic, language, and cultural backgrounds. Child-rearing patterns and parenting styles vary both within and across the different groups. That is as it should be. Variety is a healthy and positive social reality. The so-called normal and healthy functional family has a broad range of appropriate definitions.

There are, however, clearly defined cases in which a child or a family is set apart and is defined as needing special treatment. All people can be affected; special cases are not related or restricted to any particular group or social class of people. Special treatment cases include:

- Dysfunctional families in which children are neglected or abused or where parents have been or are involved in substance abuse

- Children who suffer from chronic illness or have a physical handicap

Child Abuse and Neglect

Young children, unfortunately, are sometimes targets for abuse and neglect by adults responsible for their care. These adults may include the parents, relatives, babysitters, child care providers, or any other adults who come into contact with the child. Abuse can occur in many forms, including physical, emotional, verbal, and sexual abuse.

Physical abuse includes hitting, shaking, and burning children and other forms of physical punishment, such as tying a child to a chair or bed, closing or locking children in a closet, and so on. Failing to provide a child with adequate food or other necessities, such as clothing, failing to change the child's diapers or clothing regularly, or leaving the child wet or soiled for long periods of time is also considered abusive. Such maltreatment can cause serious illness or create unhealthy conditions as well as physical discomfort for the child.

Emotional abuse includes not providing the child with adequate nurturing, warmth, or appropriate care and supervision. Willful emotional neglect and withdrawal of appropriate care and supervision are also forms of emotional abuse.

Verbal abuse is excessive yelling, taunting, and teasing.

Sexual abuse implies adult sexual behavior that exploits a child by actions such as fondling or exposing genitals or by performing sexual acts with a child.

Suspicious Injuries and Unusual Behaviors

As a caregiver, you may notice bruises, burns, or other injuries on children in your care that seem slightly (or grossly) suspicious. Injuries that are recurrent or unexplained or do not make sense for the child's particular age are all signs of possible abuse. Those injuries are not the ordinary scraped knees of beginning walkers or the bumps and bangs of new crawlers. Injuries that indicate possible abuse oftentimes appear in places that are not usually bumped or banged, such as on the child's back or abdomen or around the genitals.

If parents' explanations of a particular injury are strange or inconsistent, you may well have cause for concern. Suspicious injuries and unusual behaviors may indicate child abuse. Sometimes the injuries are coupled with unusual behavior on the part of the child. Some abused children are especially withdrawn; others act out a great deal and have very difficult behavior. Some children may be overly tuned-in to adults and adults' feelings and may seem wary of adults; such children are anxious, scared, or even cautiously trying to please every adult in sight.

Sexually abused children oftentimes act out adult sexual behaviors that generally are unknown to young children unless they have learned them from older children or adults. Other specific physical signs of sexual abuse may include difficulty sitting or walking because of pain, itching, or bruises around the rectal or genital area; bloody or stained undergarments; regressive soiling or wetting the pants or bed. Behavioral signs are similar to those listed above for other types of abuse.

The Caregiver's Legal Obligation

Child abuse is obviously a very serious matter. It is important to protect a child from abusing adults. In most states your legal obligation as a caregiver is quite clear: *it is imperative that you report suspected child abuse.* You do not have to prove you are right; all you have to do is suspect abuse. When you suspect abuse, you should call either the police or the local Child Protective Services (CPS) agency and report your suspicions. In most states the agency will ask you to file a written report (also a legal obligation), and then the agency will follow up with an investigation in cases it deems necessary.

For further guidelines to help you decide when something is suspicious enough for you to report, see *Child Abuse Prevention Handbook,* published by the Office of the Attorney General in Sacramento. Another helpful resource is *Making a Difference,* a handbook

Suspicious injuries and unusual behaviors may indicate child abuse.

and videotape training package for child care providers published by the California Child Care Resource and Referral Network in San Francisco.

A full understanding of the complexities of child abuse and neglect is important for everyone who works in child care. The topic should be included periodically in preservice and in-service training for both child care providers and parents.

Some children may arrive in your care unwashed, unfed, unchanged—and you may suspect their condition is the result of parental neglect. It is important to determine whether the child is truly neglected or the parents' perception of good care simply differs from yours. The care may be adequate but different from what you would provide. Also important is to take cultural differences into consideration. For example, differences in care may stem from differences in cultural values and beliefs. However, if the child is truly suffering from parental neglect, it must be reported for the good of the child.

If you suspect child abuse, you should report it.

The Abused Child's Need for Trust

The task of the infant during the first year is to establish trust. Usually, that happens automatically as attachment grows, needs are met in a timely fashion, and the infant comes to see the world as a friendly, safe place. Abused infants and toddlers may not develop a sense of basic trust if they lack attachment, if they are battered, or if they are neglected. Although you have little control over the lives of abused children when they are not in your care, you can concentrate on doing your best to meet their needs when they are in your care.

The following tips help young or mobile infants to develop trust:

1. Provide a consistent, predictable environment.

Abused infants and toddlers may not develop a sense of basic trust if they lack attachment, if they are battered, or if they are neglected.

2. Respond quickly to any indication that the child needs something. Do not make him or her wait too long to be fed or changed.

3. Help the child establish an attachment in the program by assigning one person, a primary caregiver, to care for the child. If the child is in care longer than the working hours of one caregiver, then a second caregiver should be assigned to the child. This approach provides children the consistency of having one person in the child care program they can count on to "attach to" and trust rather than the unpredictability of never knowing who will care for them. By consistently being always the same person to engage in caregiving routines, such as feeding and diapering, the primary caregiver will come to know each child's unique temperament, behavioral characteristics, and personality. The caregiver, like the infant, will form an attachment—each one to the other.

4. Support parents rather than blame them. That is hard to do but important when you are dealing with a suffering infant. Parents batter or neglect because they are not able to get their own needs met. Parents, too, need help and support.

5. Use the authorities and experts available to you for support and for advice on how to handle the child, the parents, and the situations that may arise.

Toddlers also may be dealing with trust issues. You can help toddlers by following the guidelines for infants. In addition, you may need to be especially understanding about difficult behavior. Toddlers who do not trust may resist naptime, for instance. They may feel vulnerable when going to sleep; therefore, they will fight against sleeping. Or perhaps the difficult behavior centers on eating. Toddlers may be particularly crabby at mealtimes. So while you are guiding and controlling the difficult behavior, think about what may be causing it.

Attachment remains a primary issue for toddlers. Although your caregiver–child ratio may be larger for the over-two age group, it is still very important that you help each toddler attach to one caregiver. As trust develops in infants, so trust grows in toddlers when they can depend on one particular person to provide for their primary care. In other words, the primary caregiving system that fosters attachment helps the toddler establish and maintain trust.

The Abused Toddler's Need for Autonomy

Abused or neglected toddlers may be stunted in their movement toward self-control and independence. *Infant/Toddler Caregiving: A Guide to Social-Emotional Growth and Socialization* gives further information about the need for autonomy as well as how to respond to that need.

You can help the abused or neglected toddler who is deficient in the area of self-control and independence by doing the following:

1. Patiently and gently teach control and provide control for the toddler when necessary. Abused toddlers may be extra aggressive with other children. You have to be firm about stopping the aggression (such as hitting, biting, hair pulling) but gentle and understanding at the same time.

2. Give special attention to the withdrawn child and help him or her become more outgoing. Encourage social interactions with other children. Encourage the child to explore the environment by providing interesting, age-appropriate toys and activities. Provide extra support for the withdrawn toddler to draw the child out of his or her shyness and insecurity.

3. Encourage the child's expression of his or her feelings. The abused or neglected child may be angry or fearful or perhaps both. Because words are limited in toddlers, actions may be the only way those feelings can be expressed. Help the toddler to use words to express feelings and describe needs and wants while you guide the child's actions so that he or she does not harm anyone or anything. Particular materials and activities in the program can be especially helpful. For example, water play, sand play, playdough, pounding boards, and dramatic play are time-honored play activities that provide a means for children to express their feelings by a soothing activity, vigorous physical play, or acting out experiences and feelings.

4. Help parents cope with and control difficult behavior in effective, nonabusive ways. Parent education can be one of your most important services if you are able to establish and maintain a positive and supportive relationship with the parent(s).

Caregivers' Reactions

Be aware of your own feelings about the abused child. Caregivers may find it difficult to like some children. These children may trigger anger in all the adults around them. Be aware of your feelings and the child's behaviors that are connected to those feelings. If you feel aggressive toward the child, put extra energy into responding in firm but *gently* controlling ways. The child may expect adults to act aggressively, to cause pain. The child's behavior may trigger urges in you to do just that. Resist those urges. Abused children have an extra need for *gentle* rather than tough control. If your negative feelings persist, seek professional support for yourself so you can confront and deal with your own feelings as well as meet the critical emotional needs of the abused child.

Substance Abuse

Babies of alcohol- and drug-addicted mothers or of mothers who used alcohol or drugs while they were pregnant are showing up more and more often in child care programs. One out of every ten pregnant women has used illegal substances during pregnancy, according to a survey taken in 1988 by the National Association for Perinatal Addiction Research and Education (NAPARE). That means at least 375,000 newborn infants each year have been exposed to potentially health-threatening drugs. "A woman who uses cocaine even once during her pregnancy can cause severe damage to the fetus, including stillbirth, spontaneous abortion, premature birth, and a wide array of problems associated with physical and neurological underdevelopment," according to an article in *The Christian Science Monitor,* February 15, 1989.[1]

Babies whose mothers abuse alcohol and drugs are showing up more and more often in child care programs.

Physical and Behavioral Characteristics

Babies born of substance abusers may have been through a lot by the time they get to you. The behaviors exhibited by babies born of substance abusers as well as the physical conditions of the babies result from and are complicated by a number of factors, such as prenatal history, prematurity, and low birth weight. The babies may also have undergone withdrawal in the first hours of life.

What are those babies like? Behavioral problems often include difficulty in sleeping. The babies may be extremely hypersensitive and irritable, cry excessively, and have outbursts of screaming. They may be especially tense, restless, hypertonic, and generally overexcitable. Jittery movements, hyperactivity, and shutting out stimulation are other common behaviors. If the parent was an intravenous drug user before or during pregnancy or both, the baby may be born with diseases such as AIDS and hepatitis. Those diseases, passed from mother to baby, are contracted from using contaminated needles.

The infants may also have been born with serious birth defects, such as mental retardation, cerebral palsy, and other physical abnormalities, such as facial, cardiac, genital, and urinary defects. These babies are also especially susceptible to stroke and sudden infant death (SID).

The babies' physical and behavioral problems related to parental substance abuse may be complicated by additional problems of the life-style at home. Frequently, substance abusers have poor nutrition and so do their infants. The substance abusers neglect self-care as well as baby care. An unstable home life with lack of consistency may be present as well. Attachment may be shaky. Parents who are substance abusers may lack basic child care information. In short, little about the parent's life may be conducive to healthy and nurturing child rearing.

If you, the caregiver, have neither knowledge of nor experience with the special behaviors and physical needs of babies affected by substance abuse, you may well wonder what to do when such a baby enters your care. Meeting children's needs can be a fulfilling activity, but the needs of babies born of substance abusers are difficult to meet. For instance, when you put the babies down to sleep, they do not sleep but cry and fuss instead. When they finally go to sleep, they wake up again before they are fully rested. The babies are sometimes so irritable that they are hard to care for and be around. Their crying and outbursts of screaming are hard on the other children in your care, too. The infants' tenseness and restlessness give the message that you cannot make them comfortable, no matter what you do.

The hardest part about relating to the babies affected by substance abuse is that the caregiving routines you use effectively with other children do not bring the same rewards and satisfactions to you or the affected infants.

Usually, difficult babies will "grow out of it," but oftentimes the infants affected by substance abuse continue to have difficulties as toddlers as well. The behaviors they exhibited as young infants may well continue and become magnified as life gets more complicated and more is required of them. For example, common behaviors may include continued irritability, easy frustration, distractibility, aggressive and impulsive behavior, hyperactivity, temper tantrums, insecure attachments, cognitive and language difficulties, and the inability to become toilet trained. Those behaviors may be a result of damage the babies were born with or a result of their unfortunate home life. Commonly the behaviors result from a combination of factors. In any case, such behaviors make caring for a young child very difficult.

The Infant's Needs

What can you do? You must do what you can to meet the infant's or toddler's needs even though neither of you ever seems satisfied. You must continue to look for ways to comfort the hard-to-comfort child. For instance, a young infant who was exposed to cocaine may be helped by being swaddled—that is, being wrapped tightly in a receiving blanket with only the head sticking out. An older child may be comforted by being held firmly and lovingly.

A young infant who was exposed to cocaine may be helped by being swaddled.

The Toddler's Needs

When the child is older and is able to move around and interact with other children, you must look for effective ways to guide behavior. You must firmly and lovingly set clear limits and guidelines for the child as well as control unacceptable behavior. Children in your care who exhibit behaviors indicative of severe emotional problems make caregiving very difficult or impossible in a group setting, especially if the behavior is seriously threatening to the child, the child's peers, or the adults in the program. *Infant/Toddler Caregiving: A Guide to Social–Emotional Growth and Socialization* will help you understand and guide in healthy and effective ways the behavior of children who have serious difficulties. In addition, parental education and support are necessary.

Of course, you cannot do the job alone—you may need to get support services for the child and the parent. Check your community resources for agencies and professionals who work therapeutically with children and families.

While you are getting support services for the child and family, do not forget yourself. Do not try to cope alone. Find help. Discuss your concerns with other staff members, your supervisors, and other caregivers. Pick up the phone book and find out which local agencies can help you.

Chronic Illnesses and Physical Handicaps

Children with a variety of special conditions can be and should be accommodated in group child care settings. Usually the best approach is to determine the appropriateness for both the individual child/family and the program on a case-by-case basis. For example, you might care for a child with chronic asthma or an infant with a cleft palate/harelip who still needs additional surgeries. In the case of the child with asthma, the child would require special monitoring for breathing difficulties or an impending attack. The child with a harelip/cleft palate would need special care in feeding until the surgical repairs had been completed. Other examples include a child with epilepsy who would need regular medication and special supervision and a child recovering from a serious illness who might need a period

Children with a variety of special conditions can be and should be accommodated in group child care settings.

of convalescence and require a special schedule with restricted activities. Each circumstance will have its own unique issues and special care needs. Parents and the health professionals working with the child and family can advise you of the special care required.

Only some of the needs of children with special conditions are different from the needs of the average child; many needs are the same. All children need attention, relationships, protection, food, toileting or changing, sleep, and sensory experiences. However, young infants with chronic diseases, medical problems, or handicapping conditions may need to learn to trust those who care for them.

If infants have been in and out of the hospital, had numerous caregivers, and been through painful medical procedures, their sense of trust may be weakened. The child care program needs to provide consistent care by a primary caregiver in a predictable environment to help the child regain or develop trust. Primary caregiving means that one person (or possibly two when the child's day is longer than the caregiver's working hours) greets and cares for the child throughout the day during all caregiving routines—providing consistent care for the infant day after day, week after week. The intention of the primary caregiving system is to provide consistent care for the infant by one adult, or at most two adults, throughout the day and throughout the child's enrollment in the particular child care program.

Chronically ill children and children with handicaps are like other children in that they have individual needs that must be met.

Mobile infants and toddlers may also have trust issues to resolve. In addition, they need opportunities for exploration and interaction with materials, objects, and peers. Perhaps some children have been protected or restricted from exploration and interaction beyond what was necessary. While they are exploring and interacting, toddlers will run into situations where they need consistent limits. Some people find it harder to be firm with chronically ill children or children with handicapping conditions. Nevertheless, special treatment beyond what the children's medical or physical conditions warrant is a disservice to those children as well as to the other children in the group.

Find out exactly what each child needs for his or her special circumstances. Perhaps the child needs to be held in certain positions to be comfortable. Or feeding may need to be done in a certain way. The child may have a special diet. Perhaps the child has little energy for exertion and may be easily overstressed; therefore, you have to restrict his or her activity level. The child may need some specialized treatment or therapy that you will have to administer. Perhaps some particular exercises are important for the child's development.

Some chronically ill children or children with particular medical conditions may have an underactive immune system. Those children need more protection than other children from ordinary germs. It is important that you educate all caregiving staff and all of the parents in the program so they fully understand the special issues of concern for the children and do not regard legitimate health concerns as arbitrary or overprotective.

Communication with parents is vital if you are to meet a child's special needs. Let the child's parent(s) know how important it is to alert you to any warning signs that may signal problems for the child. A special health history form is important for recording information, including medications or treatments to be administered, special instructions on how to carry out caregiving routines in ways that meet the child's special needs, monitoring requirements, behavioral characteristics related to the condition, possible side effects of medications, and what constitutes an emergency as well as instructions about how to handle it.

Points to Consider

1. Are you able to look at all children under your care as children first and children with conditions, histories, or problems second? If not, do you have some ideas about how to change that situation?

2. Do you have some ideas about how to keep the atmosphere as caring and pleasant as possible even when the behaviors of a particular child work against that?

3. Do you know how to determine what each child in your program needs?

4. How much do you know about changing behaviors? Do you have some ideas about how to increase your knowledge?

5. How much do you know about the outside resources available to you, to the children in your program, and to their families?

Note

1. "Crack Babies: U.S. Health-care Crisis in the Making," *The Christian Science Monitor*, February 15, 1989.

Suggested Resources

Books and Articles

Child Abuse Prevention Handbook. Sacramento: Office of the Attorney General, 1985.

Provides an overview of the laws, practices, and procedures for preventing, detecting, reporting, and treating child abuse.

Fauvre, M. "Including Young Children with 'New' Chronic Illnesses in an Early Childhood Education Setting," *Young Children*, Vol. 43 (1988), 71–78.

Discusses how teachers can respond to children with chronic disease or medical conditions. Gives practical information for older children that can be applied easily to infants and toddlers.

Infant and Toddler Program Quality Review Instrument. Sacramento: California State Department of Education, 1988.

Provides guidelines for assessing the quality of programs for infants and toddlers.

Making a Difference. San Francisco: California Child Care Resource and Referral Network, 1986.

Created specifically for caregivers. Provides information on preventing and reporting child abuse and neglect.

Infant/Toddler Caregiving: A Guide to Social–Emotional Growth and Socialization. Sacramento: California State Department of Education, 1990.

Visions for Infant/Toddler Care: Guidelines for Professional Caregiving. Sacramento: California State Department of Education, 1988.

Presents goals or visions for quality care of infants and toddlers, which should be considered by caregivers and directors of child care.

Audiovisuals

Getting in Tune: Creating Nurturing Relationships with Infants and Toddlers. Child Care Video Magazine. Sacramento: California State Department of Education, 1988. Videocassette, color, 24 minutes; printed guide.

Presents the "responsive process," which includes three steps: watching, asking, and adapting. Helps the caregiver learn what a young child needs and how best to respond to that need.

Human Development: A New Look at the Infant—Attachment (Program 5). Irvine, Calif.: Concept Media, 1983. Videocassette or filmstrip/sound cassette, color, 27 minutes; printed guide.

Reviews Mary Ainsworth's work in the area of attachment. Discusses attachment behaviors and the role they play in separations and reunions. Explores the importance of caregiver sensitivity. Available from Concept Media, P.O. Box 19542, Irvine, CA 92713-9542.

Respectfully Yours: Magda Gerber's Approach to Professional Infant/Toddler Care. Child Care Video Magazine. Sacramento: California State Department of Education, 1988. Videocassette, color, 55 minutes; printed guide.

Presents Magda Gerber's philosophy based on respecting the baby.

Summary of Questions About Caregiving Routines

1. Are you paying attention to the social–emotional climate of caregiving routines? Are you aware of what it is like (for child, parent, and caregiver) when the caregiver does and does not take into consideration the affective (emotional) side of routines?

2. Do you give attention to the age, stage, and developmental level of the children during caregiving routines and adjust accordingly?

3. Do you use routines as opportunities for one-to-one interactions between you and individual children?

4. Do you consistently promote health and safety during the planning and carrying out of all routines?

5. Is what you do during routines consistent with your program's goals and philosophy? Do you integrate routines into the program structure?

6. What do you understand about the relationship of early caregiving routines to the habits and attitudes the child carries into later life?

7. What do you understand about the relation of your routines to the individual child's family life? How well does the way you carry out routines fit with the way the child's family carries out routines? Do your program goals and philosophy fit with the child's family's goals and philosophy?

8. How consistent are the routines within your program? Does the child experience a consistent approach from all caregivers who carry out routines with him or her?

9. How do routines as performed in your program contribute to the caregiver's development, convenience, and renewal?

Appendix

A. Information Sheet

B. Identification and Emergency Information

C. Accident Sheet

D. Physician's Report Form—Day Care Centers

E. Child's Preadmission Health History—Parent's Report

F. Child's Preadmission Health History—Parent's Report (Extended Version)

G. Medication Release

H. Infant Diet/Meal Plan

I. Exposure Notices

Information Sheet

Date _____

Baby's Name

_____

Feedings

_____

Sleep

_____

Diapers or Toileting Information

_____

Other

_____

Comments

IDENTIFICATION AND EMERGENCY INFORMATION
DAY CARE CENTERS

To Be Completed by Parent or Guardian

CHILD'S NAME	LAST	MIDDLE	FIRST	SEX	TELEPHONE ( )
ADDRESS	NUMBER	STREET	CITY	STATE	ZIP	BIRTHDATE

FATHER'S NAME	LAST	MIDDLE	FIRST	BUSINESS TELEPHONE ( )
HOME ADDRESS	NUMBER	STREET	CITY	STATE	ZIP	HOME TELEPHONE ( )

MOTHER'S NAME	LAST	MIDDLE	FIRST	BUSINESS TELEPHONE ( )
HOME ADDRESS	NUMBER	STREET	CITY	STATE	ZIP	HOME TELEPHONE ( )

PERSON RESPONSIBLE FOR CHILD	LAST NAME	MIDDLE	FIRST	HOME TELEPHONE ( )	BUSINESS TELEPHONE ( )

ADDITIONAL PERSONS WHO MAY BE CALLED IN EMERGENCY

NAME	ADDRESS	TELEPHONE	RELATIONSHIP

PHYSICIAN OR DENTIST TO BE CALLED IN EMERGENCY

PHYSICIAN	ADDRESS	MEDICAL PLAN AND NUMBER	TELEPHONE ( )
DENTIST	ADDRESS	MEDICAL PLAN AND NUMBER	TELEPHONE ( )

IF PHYSICIAN CANNOT BE REACHED, WHAT ACTION SHOULD BE TAKEN?

☐ CALL EMERGENCY HOSPITAL   ☐ OTHER   EXPLAIN _____

NAMES OF PERSONS AUTHORIZED TO TAKE CHILD FROM THE FACILITY
(CHILD WILL NOT BE ALLOWED TO LEAVE WITH ANY OTHER PERSON WITHOUT WRITTEN AUTHORIZATION FROM PARENT OR GUARDIAN)

NAME	RELATIONSHIP

TIME CHILD WILL BE CALLED FOR

SIGNATURE OF PARENT OR GUARDIAN	DATE

TO BE COMPLETED BY FACILITY DIRECTOR/ADMINISTRATOR

DATE OF ADMISSION	DATE LEFT

LIC 700 (8 86) (CONFIDENTIAL)

86 41957

Accident Sheet

Date	Time	Child's Name	Location	Accident	Action Taken	Initials

PHYSICIAN'S REPORT—DAY CARE CENTERS
(CHILD'S PRE-ADMISSION HEALTH EVALUATION)

STATEMENT TO PHYSICIAN

_____ , born _____ is being studied for readiness to enter
(NAME OF CHILD)   (BIRTH DATE)

_____ . This Day Care Center provides a program which extends from _____ : _____
(NAME OF DAY CARE CENTER)

a.m. to _____ : _____ , _____ days a week. The daily activities include vigorous outdoor play.

The schedule includes morning and afternoon snacks, a noon meal, and a nap after lunch.

Please provide a report on above-named child using the form below. I hereby authorize release of medical information contained in this report to the above-named Day Care Center.

_____   _____
(SIGNATURE OF PARENT, GUARDIAN, OR OTHER RESPONSIBLE PARTY)   (DATE)

PHYSICIAN'S REPORT

Above-named child ☐ is ☐ is not   physically and emotionally able to participate in the Day Care Center described above.

COMMENTS:

_____

_____

ANY PHYSICAL CONDITIONS REQUIRING SPECIAL ATTENTION IN THE DAY CARE CENTER:

_____

_____

_____

MEDICATION PRESCRIBED OR SPECIAL ROUTINES WHICH SHOULD BE INCLUDED IN THE DAY CARE CENTER FOR CHILD'S CTIVITIES:

	TYPE *	DATE GIVEN	GIVEN BY	DATE READ	READ BY	mm INDUR.	IMPRESSION	TYPE *	DATE GIVEN	GIVEN BY	DATE READ	READ BY	mm INDUR.	IMPRESSION
TB SKIN TESTS	☐ PPD-Mantoux ☐ Other						☐ Pos ☐ Neg	☐ PPD-Mantoux ☐ Other						☐ Pos ☐ Neg
	☐ PPD-Mantoux ☐ Other						☐ Pos ☐ Neg	☐ PPD-Mantoux ☐ Other						☐ Pos ☐ Neg

CHEST X-RAY   Impression: ☐ normal ☐ abnormal   Signature /
(Necessary if skin test positive)   Film date: ____ / ____ / ____   Person is free of communicable tuberculosis ☐ yes ☐ no   Agency _____

* If required for school entry, must be Mantoux unless exception granted by local health department.

DOES CHILD HAVE ANY OBVIOUS OCULAR ABNORMALITIES?

_____

DOES VISION SEEM TO BE ADEQUATE IN EACH EYE?

_____

IMMUNIZATION HISTORY: (If a completed yellow "California Immunization Record, PM-298" is enclosed, this section need not be filled out.)

VACCINE	Date each dose was given (month and year at a minimum)				
	1st	**2nd**	**3rd**	**4th**	**5th**
Polio					
DTP or Td					
Measles					
Rubella		PHYSICIAN'S SIGNATURE (OR PHYSICIAN ASSISTANT/NURSE PRACTITIONER)			
Mumps		ADDRESS			
Hib (Haemophilus Influenza Type b)		TELEPHONE ( )		DATE	

LIC 701 (7/89) (Confidential)

119

CHILD'S PREADMISSION HEALTH HISTORY—PARENT'S REPORT

CHILD'S NAME		SEX	BIRTH DATE

FATHER'S NAME	DOES FATHER LIVE IN HOME WITH CHILD?

MOTHER'S NAME	DOES MOTHER LIVE IN HOME WITH CHILD?

IS /HAS CHILD BEEN UNDER REGULAR SUPERVISION OF PHYSICIAN?	DATE OF LAST PHYSICAL/MEDICAL EXAMINATION

DEVELOPMENTAL HISTORY   *Not applicable to school-age children.

WALKED AT* MONTHS	BEGAN TALKING AT* MONTHS	TOILET TRAINING STARTED AT* MONTHS

PAST ILLNESSES — Check illnesses that child has had and specify approximate dates of illnesses:

	DATES		DATES		DATES
☐ Chicken Pox		☐ Diabetes		☐ Poliomyelitis	
☐ Asthma		☐ Epilepsy		☐ Ten Day Measles (Rubeola)	
☐ Rheumatic Fever		☐ Whooping cough		☐ Three Day Measles (Rebella)	
☐ Hay Fever		☐ Mumps			

SPECIFY ANY OTHER SERIOUS OR SEVERE ILLNESSES OR ACCIDENTS

DOES CHILD HAVE FREQUENT COLDS? ☐ YES ☐ NO	HOW MANY IN LAST YEAR?	LIST ANY ALLERGIES STAFF SHOULD BE AWARE OF

DAILY ROUTINES   *Not applicable to school-age children.

WHAT TIME DOES CHILD GET UP?*	WHAT TIME DOES CHILD GO TO BED?*	DOES CHILD SLEEP WELL?*
DOES CHILD SLEEP DURING THE DAY?*	WHEN?*	HOW LONG?*

DIET PATTERN: (What does child usually eat for these meals?)	BREAKFAST	WHAT ARE USUAL EATING HOURS?
	NOON MEAL	BREAKFAST _____ LUNCH_____ DINNER
	EVENING MEAL	

ANY FOOD DISLIKES?	ANY EATING PROBLEMS?

ARE BOWEL MOVEMENTS REGULAR? ☐ YES ☐ NO	WHAT IS USUAL TIME?*
WORD USE FOR "BOWELL MOVEMENT":	URINATION*

PARENTS EVALUATION OF CHILDS HEALTH

PARENT'S EVALUATION OF CHILD'S PERSONALITY

HOW DOES CHILD GET ALONG WITH PARENTS, BROTHERS, SISTERS AND OTHER CHILDREN?

HAS THE CHILD HAD GROUP PLAY EXPERIENCES?

DOES THE CHILD HAVE ANY SPECIAL PROBLEMS—FEARS? (EXPLAIN)

WHAT IS PLAN FOR CARE WHEN CHILD IS ILL?

REASON FOR REQUESTING DAY CARE PLACEMENT

PARENT'S SIGNATURE	DATE

LIC 702 (1/90)(CONFIDENTIAI)

90 55707

Child's Preadmission Health History

Parent's Report (Extended Version)

Name of Child _____ Birth Date _____ Sex _____

Father _____ Age _____ Living in home with child? _____

Mother _____ Age _____ Living in home with child? _____

Medical Information

Has child been under regular supervision of a physician? _____

Date of last physical examination _____

Date and results of last hearing examination _____

Any speech problems? _____ Is the child seeing a speech therapist? _____

If so, who? _____

Past Illnesses: Check those child has had—give approximate dates.

☐ Chicken Pox _____   ☐ Asthma _____   ☐ Poliomyelitis _____

☐ Hay Fever _____   ☐ Epilepsy _____   ☐ Whooping Cough _____

☐ Diabetes _____   ☐ Three-Day "German" Measles (Rubella) _____

☐ Rheumatic Fever _____   ☐ Ten-Day Measles (Rubeola) _____

☐ Mumps _____   ☐ Other serious or severe illnesses or accidents? _____

_____

Any physical limitations of the child? _____

Current status of family health (including any serious health problems of other family members) _____

_____

_____

Prenatal health of mother with this child and number of this pregnancy. Were there any complications during

labor or delivery? Any abnormalities noted at birth? _____

_____

Birth Weight _____ Birth Height _____

Any bone or joint problems? _____

Any convulsions? _____

What do you feel is the best thing about your child's behavior? _____

_____

Is there anything about your child's behavior that worries you? _____

_____

What rules does your family have for behavior at home? _____

_____

What have you found is the best way to get your child to do what you want him/her to do? _____

_____

In your opinion, is your child more active than the average child, less active, average? _____

What are your feelings about the following: aggression, punishment, curiosity about sex, sex roles, going

barefoot, racial concern? _____

_____

What is your child's favorite activity? _____

Has your child begun playing with other children? _____

Does your child prefer playing with a group of friends or just one or two? _____

If your child has a choice, will he/she spend most of his/her free time with friends or alone? _____

Are there any things your child really dislikes having done to him/her (e.g., being tickled, being playfully

swung in the air)? _____

Are there any things your child is afraid of? _____

Has your child had any really frightening experiences? _____

Ages of other children in the home_____

Plan for care when child is ill:

    If illness begins at home? _____

    If illness begins at school? _____

How does your child act when "coming down" with a cold? _____

What is the usual procedure when your child is fussy? _____

_____   _____
          Parent/Guardian Signature   Date

Medication Release

Date _____

Parent's Instructions—Children receiving medication at a child care facility must have:

1. Original prescription bottle with drug name, date, child's name, prescribing physician's name, dosage, and times to be given.

2. Written consent from parent permitting child care facility personnel to give medication to child and specifying times per day to be given.

3. Any medication which is to be given for longer than two weeks must have the physician's written instructions as well as signature in addition to the parent's signature.

Name of child _____

Name of medication _____

Dosage _____ Times to be given _____

I hereby authorize the child care personnel to assist in the administration of medications described above from

_____ until _____
          (Date)   (Date)

_____   _____
       (Parent's signature)   (Date)

- -

Physician's Release—Required for any medication given for longer than a two-week period.

Diagnosis _____

Name of medication and dosage _____

Times to be given per day _____

Length of time to be given _____

_____   _____
      (Physician's signature)   (Date)

Infant Diet/Meal Plan

Name _____

Birthdate _____

Foods already introduced:

Type of formula _____

Breast-fed? ☐ Yes   ☐ No

Schedule for introducing new foods:

Baby's Age   Food

_____   _____
Parent's signature   Caregiver's signature

California

Dear Parents: Revised 4/85

On _____ your child may have been exposed to the disease that is checked below. The information contained below does not replace consultation with your physician if your child is sick.

OTHER REPORTABLE ILLNESSES THAT DO NOT CAUSE RASH - Report to Health Protection (Phone: 299-5858)

( )   HEMOPHILUS INFECTIONS—Onset usually 2-7 days after exposure. Symptoms include fever, vomiting, headache, sleepiness, irritability or stiff neck. Sometimes severe sore throat and breathing difficulty occurs. This is a very serious illness; consult your physician promptly if symptoms occur.

( )   HEPATITIS A (infectious hepatitis)—Onset 2-6 weeks after exposure. Symptoms may include nausea, vomiting, abdominal pain, loss of appetite, dark urine and yellowing of the skin and eyes. Symptoms are usually more severe in adults than in children.

( )   MENINGOCOCCAL MENINGITIS—Onset usually 2-5 days after exposure. Symptoms include fever, vomiting, headache, sleepiness, irritability, or a stiff neck. This is a very serious illness; consult your physician promptly if symptoms occur.

Consult your physician or the Health Department regarding preventive measures for contacts to these illnesses.

INFECTIOUS DIARRHEAS

( )   CAMPYLOBACTER—Onset 1-10 days after exposure. Symptoms include fever, abdominal pain, nausea, vomiting and diarrhea. The diarrhea may be foul-smelling and bloody. Consult your physician for treatment. Children may return to school after treatment and when diarrhea has ended.

( )   CRYPTOSPORIDIOSIS—Onset 5-10 days after exposure. Symptoms include abdominal pain, nausea, occasional vomiting and watery diarrhea. The diarrhea may continue for up to 2 weeks. Children may return to school when the diarrhea ends.

( )   GIARDIA—Onset is 1-4 weeks after exposure. The symptoms include abdominal pain, bloating and diarrhea. The diarrhea may be foul-smelling and greasy. Consult your physician for treatment if symptoms occur. Children may return to school when the diarrhea stops and when cleared by the county Health Department.

( )   SALMONELLA—Onset 1-3 days after exposure. Symptoms include fever, abdominal pain, and diarrhea. The diarrhea may contain blood or mucus. Consult your physician for treatment. Children in Day Care may return to school only when cleared by the county Health Department.

( )   SHIGELLA—Onset 1-7 days after exposure. Symptoms include fever, abdominal pain and diarrhea. The diarrhea may contain blood or mucus. Consult your physician for treatment. Children in Day Care may return only when cleared by the county Health Department.

HANDWASHING PREVENTS SPREAD OF THESE DISEASES.   125

County of Santa Clara
California

Health Department
2220 Moorpark Avenue
San Jose, California 95128

EXPOSURE NOTICE

Dear Parents:

Revised 4/85

On _____ your child may have been exposed to the disease that is checked below. The information contained below does not replace consultation with your physician if your child is sick.

VACCINE PREVENTABLE ILLNESS - Unimmunized contacts should consult their physician. Additional cases of these diseases should be reported to Immunization Assistance Program. (Phone: 299-6850)

( )   GERMAN MEASLES (Rubella) — Onset about 2 weeks after exposure. Symptoms include "cold symptoms", swollen glands at the back of the neck, and pinkish-red rash. The child may return to school 5 days after the onset of the rash. This disease may be dangerous to pregnant women who are not immune.

( )   MEASLES (Rubeola) — Onset 1-2 weeks after exposure. Symptoms include runny nose, watery eyes, cough and fever. A rash appears on about the third or fourth day of illness. The child may return to school 5 days after the appearance of the rash. If measles occurs consult your physician for advice.

( )   MUMPS — Onset 2-3 weeks after exposure. Symptoms include pain in cheeks which may be increased when chewing; swelling may occur over the jaw in front of the ear. Abdominal pain may occur. Children may return to school when the swelling is gone.

( )   WHOOPING COUGH (Pertussis) — Onset 7-10 days after exposure. Early symptoms include a tight cough which becomes more severe within 1-2 weeks. Children may vomit or make whooping sounds during severe coughing episodes. Children may return to school after 1 week of treatment with antibiotics.

OTHER REPORTABLE ILLNESS THAT CAUSE RASH - Report to Immunization Assistance Program. (Phone: 299-6850)

( )   CHICKEN POX (Varicella) — Onset about 2-3 weeks after exposure. Symptoms include fever and irritability and a rash. The rash resembles small blisters which appear first on the trunk, then on the face. The child may return to school 7 days after onset of rash and if all of the blisters are dry.

( )   "FIFTH DISEASE" (Erythema Infectiosum) — Onset about 1-2 weeks after exposure. A mild illness that starts with a rash on the face that resembles "slapped Cheeks".

( )   SCABIES — Onset 2-6 weeks after exposure. Symptoms include itching and a very contagious rash occurring around fingers, wrists, elbows, underarms, waist, thighs, or ankles. Consult your physician for diagnosis and treatment if symptoms occur.

( )   STREPTOCOCCAL INFECTIONS:
   ( )   STREP THROAT — Onset 1-4 days after exposure. Includes fever, sore throat, and may also include abdominal pain. Consult your physician for treatment. Children may return to school after 2 days of antibiotic treatment.

   ( )   SCARLET FEVER — Similar to strep throat but child also has a fine rash on face and body. The rash is rough and may feel like sandpaper. Consult your physician for treatment.

   ( )   IMPETIGO — A strep infection of the skin which causes areas of skin infection which may be oozing or crusted. Consult physician for treatment.

County of Santa Clara

California

EXPOSURE NOTICE

Dear Parents:

On _____ your child may have been exposed to the disease that is checked below. The information contained below does not replace consultation with your physician if your child is sick.

NON-REPORTABLE ILLNESSES OF CONCERN - Consult your private physician.

( ) HEAD LICE (Pediculosis capitis)—Lice may spread from person to person after close contact. Lice do not jump or fly. The primary symptom is itching of the scalp or back of the neck. Sometimes nits (small white eggs) can be seen on the hair shafts. Treatment for lice may be obtained from a pharmacy or physician. Children may return to school after treatment is completed.

( ) PINK EYE (Conjunctivitis)—Eyes are red and crusted with mucus discharge. There are many causes for this disorder. If symptoms occur consult your physician for treatment. Children may return to school when the infection has cleared.

( ) PINWORMS—A mild infection characterized by rectal or vaginal itching; abdominal pain is uncommon. Consult your physician if symptoms occur.

Revised 4/85

Publications Available from the Department of Education

This publication is a component of The Program for Infant/Toddler Caregivers, a comprehensive training system for caregivers of infants and toddlers. Other available materials developed for this program include the following:

ISBN	Title (Date of publication)	Price
0-8011-0751-2	First Moves: Welcoming a Child to a New Caregiving Setting (videocassette and guide) (1988)*	$65.00
0-8011-0839-x	Flexible, Fearful, or Feisty: The Different Temperaments of Infants and Toddlers (videocassette and guide) (1990)*	65.00
0-8011-0809-8	Getting in Tune: Creating Nurturing Relationships with Infants and Toddlers (videocassette and guide) (1990)*	65.00
0-8011-0767-9	Infant and Toddler Program Quality Review Instrument (1988)	2.00
0-8011-0878-0	Infant/Toddler Caregiving: A Guide to Creating Partnerships with Parents (1990)	8.25
0-8011-0880-2	Infant/Toddler Caregiving: A Guide to Language Development and Communication (1990)	8.25
0-8011-0877-2	Infant/Toddler Caregiving: A Guide to Routines (1990)	8.25
0-8011-0879-9	Infant/Toddler Caregiving: A Guide to Setting Up Environments (1990)	8.25
0-8011-0876-4	Infant/Toddler Caregiving: A Guide to Social-Emotional Growth and Socialization (1990)	8.25
0-8011-0750-4	Infant/Toddler Caregiving: An Annotated Guide to Media Training Materials (1989)	8.75
0-8011-0869-1	It's Not Just Routine: Feeding, Diapering, and Napping Infants and Toddlers (videocassette and guide) (1990)*	65.00
0-8011-0753-9	Respectfully Yours: Magda Gerber's Approach to Professional Infant/Toddler Care (videocassette and guide) (1988)*	65.00
0-8011-0752-0	Space to Grow: Creating a Child Care Environment for Infants and Toddlers (videocassette and guide) (1988)*	65.00
0-8011-0758-x	Visions for Infant/Toddler Care: Guidelines for Professional Caregiving (1988)	5.50

There are almost 700 publications that are available from the California Department of Education. Some of the other more recent publications or those most widely used are the following:

ISBN	Title (Date of publication)	Price
0-8011-0853-5	California Public School Directory (1990)	$14.00
0-8011-0760-1	Celebrating the National Reading Initiative (1989)	6.75
0-8011-0867-5	The Changing Language Arts Curriculum: A Booklet for Parents (1990)†	10 for 5.00
0-8011-0777-6	The Changing Mathematics Curriculum: A Booklet for Parents (1989)†	10 for 5.00
0-8011-0856-x	English as a Second Language Handbook for Adult Education Instructors (1990)	4.50
0-8011-0041-0	English–Language Arts Framework for California Public Schools (1987)	3.00
0-8011-0731-8	English–Language Arts Model Curriculum Guide, K—8 (1988)	3.00
0-8011-0804-7	Foreign Language Framework for California Public Schools (1989)	5.50
0-8011-0735-0	Here They Come: Ready or Not—Appendixes to the Full Report of the School Readiness Task Force (1988)	22.50
0-8011-0737-7	Here They Come: Ready or Not—Report of the School Readiness Task Force (Summary) (1988)	2.00
0-8011-0734-2	Here They Come: Ready or Not—Report of the School Readiness Task Force (Full Report) (1988)	4.25
	Here They Come: Ready or Not—Teleconference: "Big Change for Small Learners" (1989)	16.50
0-8011-0712-1	History–Social Science Framework for California Public Schools (1988)	6.00
0-8011-0782-2	Images: A Workbook for Enhancing Self-esteem and Promoting Career Preparation, Especially for Black Girls (1989)	6.00
0-8011-0466-1	Instructional Patterns: Curriculum for Parenthood Education (1985)	12.00
0-8011-0762-8	Moral and Civic Education and Teaching About Religion (1988)	3.25
0-8011-0303-7	A Parent's Handbook on California Education (1986)	3.25
0-8011-0667-2	Parent Involvement Programs in California (1987)	3.50
0-8011-0311-8	Recommended Readings in Literature, K—8 (1986)	2.25
0-8011-0863-z	Recommended Readings in Literature: Kindergarten Through Grade Eight, Addendum (1990)	2.25
0-8011-0745-8	Recommended Readings in Literature, K—8, Annotated Edition (1988)	4.50
0-8011-0765-2	School-Age Parenting and Infant Development Program Quality Review Instrument (1988)	2.00
0-8011-0855-1	Strengthening the Arts in California Schools: A Design for the Future (1990)	4.75
0-8011-0846-2	Toward a State of Esteem (1990)	4.00
0-8011-0805-5	Visual and Performing Arts Framework for California Public Schools (1989)	6.00
0-8011-0270-7	Young and Old Together: A Resource Directory of Intergenerational Resources (1986)	3.00

Orders should be directed to:

California Department of Education
P.O. Box 271
Sacramento, CA 95802-0271

Please include the International Standard Book Number (ISBN) for each title ordered.

Remittance or purchase order must accompany order. Purchase orders without checks are accepted only from governmental agencies. Sales tax should be added to all orders from California purchasers.

A complete list of publications available from the Department, including apprenticeship instructional materials, may be obtained by writing to the address listed above or by calling (916) 445-1260.

*Videocassette also available in Chinese (Cantonese) and Spanish at the same price.
†The price for 100 booklets is $30; the price for 1,000 booklets is $230.

88-102 6-90 5M